Restoring Prosperity

Budget Choices
for Economic Growth

**A Statement by the Research and Policy Committee
of the Committee for Economic Development**

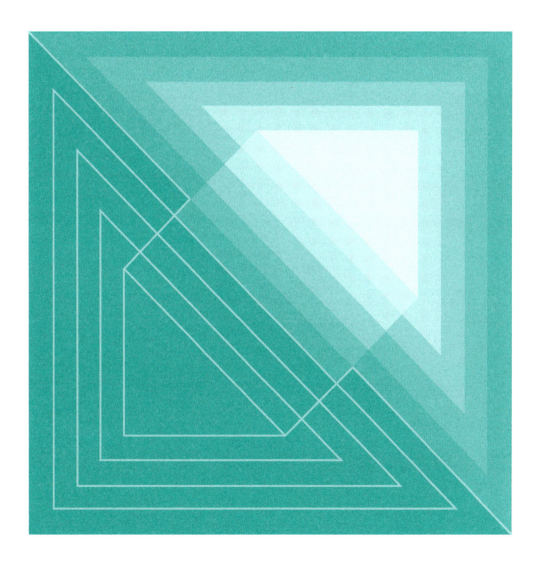

Library of Congress Cataloging-in-Publication Data

Committee for Economic Development. Research and Policy Committee. Restoring
Prosperity: Budget Choices for Economic Growth: a statement by the Research and
Policy Committee for the Committee for Economic Development.
   p. cm.
   Includes bibliographical references.
   ISBN 0-87186-095-3 : $14.50
   1. Budget deficits — United States. 2. Fiscal policy — United States. 3. Industrial
productivity — United States. 4. Saving and Investment — United States.   I. Title.
HJ2051.C64 1992
338.973--dc20   92-35947
                                                                CIP

First printing in bound-book form: 1992
Paperback: $14.50
Printed in the United States of America
Design: Rowe & Ballantine

COMMITTEE FOR ECONOMIC DEVELOPMENT
477 Madison Avenue, New York, N.Y. 10022
(212) 688-2063

2000 L Street, N.W., Washington, D.C. 20006
(202) 296-5860

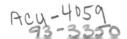

CONTENTS

Restoring Prosperity
Budget Choices
for Economic Growth

RESPONSIBILITY FOR CED STATEMENTS ON NATIONAL POLICY

The Committee for Economic Development is an independent research and educational organization of some 250 business leaders and educators. CED is nonprofit, nonpartisan, and nonpolitical. Its purpose is to propose policies that bring about steady economic growth at high employment and reasonably stable prices, increased productivity and living standards, greater and more equal opportunity for every citizen, and improved quality of life for all.

All CED policy recommendations must have the approval of trustees on the Research and Policy Committee. This committee is directed under the bylaws which emphasize that "all research is to be thoroughly objective in character, and the approach in each instance is to be from the standpoint of the general welfare and not from that of any special political or economic group." The committee is aided by a Research Advisory Board of leading social scientists and by a small permanent professional staff.

The Research and Policy Committee does not attempt to pass judgment on any pending specific legislative proposals; its purpose is to urge careful consideration of the objectives set forth in this statement and of the best means of accomplishing those objectives.

Each statement is preceded by extensive discussions, meetings, and exchange of memoranda. The research is undertaken by a subcommittee, assisted by advisors chosen for their competence in the field under study.

The full Research and Policy Committee participates in the drafting of recommendations. Likewise, the trustees on the drafting subcommittee vote to approve or disapprove a policy statement, and they share with the Research and Policy Committee the privilege of submitting individual comments for publication.

Except for the members of the Research and Policy Committee and the responsible subcommittee, the recommendations presented herein are not necessarily endorsed by other trustees or by the advisors, contributors, staff members, or others associated with CED.

RESEARCH AND POLICY COMMITTEE

---

*Voted to approve the policy statement but submitted memoranda of comment, reservation, or dissent. (See page 56.)
†Disapproved publication of this statement. (See page 56.)

SUBCOMMITTEE ON THE FEDERAL BUDGET AND ECONOMIC GROWTH

ADVISORS

WILLIAM J. BAUMOL
Department of Economics
New York University

RUDOLPH G. PENNER
Senior Manager and Director
    of Economic Studies
Policy Economics Group
KPMG Peat Marwick

PROJECT DIRECTOR

VAN DOORN OOMS
Senior Vice President and Director
    of Research
CED

PROJECT EDITOR

JULIE A. WON
Assistant Director of Information
CED

SENIOR PROJECT ADVISOR

WILLIAM J. BEEMAN
Vice President and Director
    of Economic Studies
CED

PROJECT ASSOCIATE

JEREMY A. LEONARD
Policy Analyst
CED

Purpose of this Statement

The purpose of this statement is to address our nation's most important economic problem — the slowdown in economic growth during the last two decades. Slow growth has drastically reduced our private opportunities; average real wages of American workers have stagnated for years. It has also limited our public resources, impaired our competitiveness, and now threatens our position of international leadership. While most public attention is now given to the painful, but temporary problem of a flagging economic recovery, our *fundamental* challenge is that of raising long-term economic growth. As we note, the costs of slower growth far outweigh and outlast those of recent economic weakness.

This policy statement therefore makes recommendations for rebuilding the foundations of a high-growth economy. It shows how the nation has, both privately and publicly, sacrificed investment in the future to demands for current consumption. It then proposes national goals for saving and investment and examines options to produce both the higher national saving required to finance stronger growth and more productive private and public investments. While these goals are challenging, we show that they are within our reach.

This statement recognizes that the new Administration and Congress may feel it necessary to deal with the weak economy with a program of economic stimulus. We argue that any stimulus program should be consistent with the objective of raising long-term economic growth, and we offer five principles for a short-term stimulus program that would ensure that consistency.

ACKNOWLEDGEMENTS

I would like to offer deepest thanks to the group of CED trustees and advisors who served on the subcommittee that prepared this report. Having served as chairman of that subcommittee, I know the high value of each member's participation in the discussion and formulation of policy recommendations. It was a personal pleasure to work with deeply committed participants on such an interesting and important project.

Special thanks must also go to Project Director Van Doorn Ooms, Project Associate Jeremy Leonard, and Project Editor Julie Won, who worked to get the analysis, facts, and words right.

Josh S. Weston
Chairman
CED Research and Policy Committee

Chapter 1

Introduction and Summary of Policy Recommendations

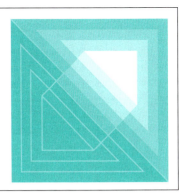

The nation stands at an economic crossroads. After two decades of slow economic growth and a prolonged stretch of recession and weak recovery, the economic discomfort and dissatisfaction of Americans was a central issue in the recent elections. A new Administration and a new Congress, with an extraordinary total of 118 new members, will take office in January with a clear message from the voters that our economic performance must improve. We have a unique opportunity to make bold policy changes to restore stronger growth. That is the good news.

The bad news is that lasting economic progress cannot be restored either immediately or painlessly. The legacy of many years of misguided policies and priorities cannot be removed without a steady and continuing effort that will require shared sacrifice. There is a danger that our resolve will weaken or that, by misunderstanding the nature of the problem, we will embrace policies that will aggravate rather than reverse our poor economic performance.

American prosperity is being threatened on two counts. The more immediate and visible problem is the painful but temporary recession and slow recovery of the past several years. This cyclical episode has been the source of much personal hardship, and although the downturn was less deep than most, the unusually slow recovery has disheartened many.

The less visible but far more serious problem is the slowdown in long-term economic growth since the early 1970s, which has held down wages and incomes. During the period 1948-1973, real hourly compensation for the American worker rose by an average of 2.9 percent per year, a rate which allows national living standards to double every generation. At the post-1973 rate, such an improvement would take a century. This slowdown will continue unless the foundations for sustained economic growth and prosperity are strengthened.

We recognize that the American people have called upon their political leaders to address both the short-term and long-term problems, and we discuss below some principles for short-term fiscal policy. But this policy statement essentially deals with the longer term. **We cannot emphasize too strongly our conviction that improving long-term growth must be the nation's top priority.** While the burden of the recession has been unequally and harshly shared, the costs of the recession for the nation as a whole pale beside those of inadequate growth. As a result of the recession, the nation has lost annual production and income of roughly $220 billion (in 1992 dollars), or $875 per capita. But the failure to sustain our historical long-term annual productivity growth of 2 percent after 1973 cost $1.4 *trillion*, or $5,400 per capita each year. This loss will continue year after year, long after the recession. We must keep the long-term goal clearly in focus and avoid any short-term palliatives that would place it in jeopardy.

FIVE PRINCIPLES FOR SHORT-TERM STIMULUS

In December 1991, CED recommended against tax cuts proposed to "jump-start" the economy because they threatened to increase future budget deficits and reduce long-term growth.[1] Although the economy has not recovered significantly from the recession, we still believe its continued weakness is not primarily cyclical but results from structural imbalances which will not be easily corrected by short-term stimulus. We remain convinced from experience that consumption-oriented tax cuts pose a grave risk to saving, investment, and economic growth.

Nevertheless, economic stagnation has now begun to undermine consumer and business confidence. Monetary policy, for reasons related to these structural problems, has been less powerful in assisting recovery than in the past. If the economy has not begun to revive when the new Administration and Congress take office in January, the economic case for stimulus will be strong and the political pressures for action will be compelling.

The danger is that short-term measures that jeopardize our longer-term future will then be enacted. However, our immediate and longer-term needs need not be in conflict if a new economic program is carefully structured. CED recommends the following five principles to guide any short-term stimulus program:

1. **The most important principle is that a stimulus program should not increase the long-term structural budget deficit.** Either its provisions should be temporary, or its future financing should be enacted in the same legislation.

2. **Short-term stimulus measures and long-term deficit reduction policies, following the principles outlined in this statement, should be integrated and legislated in a single program.** This would establish the credibility of the long-term policy and minimize the risk of an adverse financial market reaction, which could negate the short-term program's stimulative effects. It would also provide stronger political incentives for enactment of the long-term program.

3. **Deficit reduction measures should be phased in on a timetable consistent with economic recovery.** However, changing the timetable for *implementation* of a long-term program should not prevent its early *enactment*.

4. **The stimulus program should emphasize private and public investments rather than**

consumption. For that reason, we do not favor personal income tax reductions, which would primarily boost consumption. An investment tax credit, on the other hand, is recommended in this statement as a long-term measure to raise productivity growth and could be structured to provide short-term stimulus as well.

5. **Public expenditures in the program should raise the nation's productive capacity.** CED believes that selected expenditures on the education of our children, the training of our workers, the maintenance and improvement of our decaying infrastructure, and the enhancement of our science and technology base can have an important role in raising long-term growth. To the extent that such expenditures can be accelerated, they may provide some useful short-term stimulus.

However, we are skeptical that large amounts of genuinely productive expenditures can be front-loaded in this way; effective investments take time to design and implement. We should *not* undertake "make-work" programs just to increase spending. Merely labeling public expenditures as "investments" does not make them productive.

We believe that a stimulus program consistent with these five principles could help the economy in the near term without reducing the saving and investment needed to raise long-term economic growth.*

RAISING LONG-TERM GROWTH

What should our longer-term economic course now be? As our newly-elected officials begin to grapple with economic policy, it is time to once more identify basic questions and solutions. What are realistic economic hopes of Americans? Why have those hopes been disappointed in recent years? And how can we realize them in the future? This policy statement tries to answer those questions.

What do we expect from our economy? Although particular answers are diverse and numerous, they reflect three fundamental concerns about ourselves, our children's future, and our nation's role. We want:

*See memorandum by ELMER B. STAATS, (page 56).

- The assurance of opportunities to improve our material living standards through ingenuity and hard work, as our parents and grandparents did;

- The knowledge that our society will pass on to the next generation an economic base that will allow them to enjoy fulfilling and rewarding lives;

- The confidence that U.S. business and workers can compete successfully in the international arena and that America will be strong enough to lead other nations in maintaining a peaceful and open global community.

The last three years of economic weakness have undoubtedly heightened concerns about realizing these aspirations. Nevertheless, we believe that both the concerns and the problems underlying them are longer-term in nature and have been building for many years; the recent recession has acted more to galva-nize these growing apprehensions than to cause them.

Figures 1 and 2 help us understand an important reason for these concerns. Figure 1 shows the growth of three broad measures of U.S. economic performance since 1973 compared with the period 1948-1973: real gross domestic product (GDP) per person, real after-tax income per person, and hourly worker compensation. Each of these measures provides a somewhat different perspective on our economic performance, but together they tell a strong and consistent story: the rapid improvement in American incomes in the quarter century after World War II slowed sharply after about 1973, especially when the additional work needed to produce those incomes is considered.[2]

What have been the costs of this slowdown? Figure 2 compares the compensation shown in Figure 1 (adjusted to a standardized full-year

Figure 1

Comparison of Growth Rates of Several Measures of Economic Performance

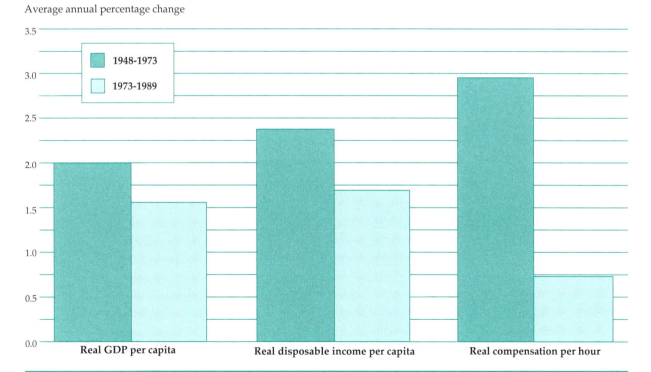

Average annual percentage change

NOTE: To avoid cyclical distortions, 1990-1991 data have been omitted.
    Real compensation per hour deflated by CPI-U-XI after 1966.
SOURCE: U.S. Departments of Commerce and Labor

basis) with what it *would have been* if compensation had continued to grow in 1973-1991 at its 1948-1973 rate of 2.9 percent — a measure suggestive of Americans' hopes and aspirations based on their families' earlier experiences. By 1991, the shortfall of the average worker's compensation below this measure was 34 percent, or about $15,500. Recognizing that the unusual 1948-1973 growth experience may have been unsustainable, Figure 2 also extrapolates 1973-1991 compensation at a rate of 2 percent. The resulting shortfall is about $8,500, or 22 percent.

It is therefore not surprising that many Americans feel frustrated and disappointed with their economic prospects. For some, this disappointment has been sharpened because total income also has become less equally distributed.* Such a trend would be of less concern were average income growing strongly, since the vast majority of families would then experience rising incomes, though at different rates. However, rising inequality combined with slow or stagnant income growth implies that many families will experience absolute as well as relative losses.[3]

Nor is it a secret that our once unrivaled international economic power is diminished. The competitive problems of key industries and ensuing job cuts are frequent front page news. We seem increasingly uncertain that we can reap fully the benefits of open international trading, of which we were the principal sponsor. We appear less able than formerly to lead the international community in the reduction of trade barriers, the coordination of economic policy, and the provision of development assistance.

Figure 2

Annualized Real Hourly Compensation
In constant 1991 dollars

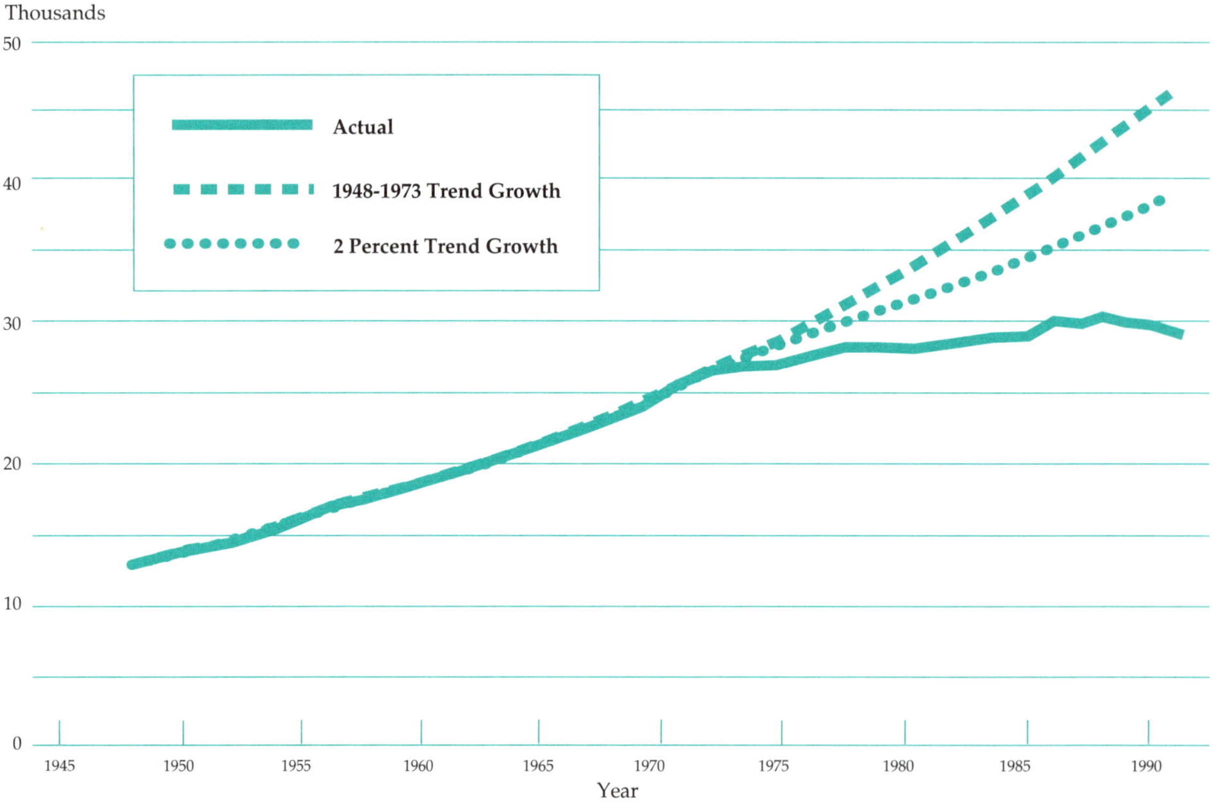

NOTE: Real compensation deflated by CPI-U-X1 after 1966.
SOURCE: U.S. Department of Commerce

*See memorandum by JAMES Q. RIORDAN, (page 56).

Finally, even the more slowly growing incomes of recent years have been secured in considerable part at the expense of future generations. We have used too much of our income, resources, and borrowing capacity — private and public — on consuming today rather than investing for tomorrow. We have slowed the development and maintenance of our infrastructure. The current taxation and spending policies of the Federal budget significantly shift the burden of financing government from ourselves to future generations.[4] In the private sector, we have not increased the stock of equipment, plant, and technology rapidly enough to raise real wages and remain fully competitive internationally.

Although it has been common to argue that the major costs of our shortsighted economic policies would harm the nation only in the future, our emphasis on consumption at the expense of saving also bears bitter fruit now. As explained in Chapter 3, the reduction in national saving during the 1980s *currently* costs us over $300 billion per year in lost output — about $1200 per person — and this cost will double by the end of the decade.

This growing gap between economic hopes and performance has led to a common view and fear that our economy is no longer capable of achieving the goals it once promised. We reject this dangerously defeatist view. We believe that our economic wounds are in large part self-inflicted and that reasonable economic expectations can be fulfilled if policy makers and citizens alike face up to the hard economic facts and remedies presented in this policy statement. We should not passively accept "the age of diminished expectations."[5] The problems are soluble; other nations in the recent past have made policy changes comparable to those required of us.

However, there are no easy or painless solutions to our problems. Many nostrums have been put forward to improve our economic future without imposing costs on ourselves today. But it is clear that a stronger economy tomorrow must entail sacrifices today. We should acknowledge explicitly and candidly this relationship between today's pain and tomorrow's gain. We must also agree that both pain and gain must be broadly and equitably shared within the society if we are to reach the political agreements necessary to travel this course successfully. By making the terms of the trade-off more explicit, we can clarify our economic goals and the choices necessary to meet them.

This policy statement first documents the stagnation of average real wages and slowdown in income growth in the last two decades, explaining how these changes in individual and family well-being were principally determined by *slower productivity growth*. The sources of productivity growth are then discussed with emphasis upon the role of *investments* in physical capital, human resources, and technology in raising productivity.

We then examine the fundamental choice facing the nation — between using growing national output to increase current consumption versus making adequate investments in the future. We show that families, businesses, and government all have been overconsuming, undersaving, and underinvesting. In spite of today's weak economy, in which the reluctance of households to spend has slowed short-term recovery in production and employment, we do not have a long-term or structural problem of inadequate consumption.

Quite the contrary. As private individuals, we have increased consumption to above 75 percent of our national income — the largest share in the last half century. Our Federal government has added to our profligacy for almost a quarter century by consistently living beyond its means. The result of those deficits is a national debt of $3 trillion — over 50 percent of our GDP and climbing — which crowds out productive investment and significantly slows growth, with the damage compounding each year.[6] We show that our government spending and tax structures tend to encourage consumption at the expense of saving and investment.

The economic danger to the nation is larger than realized because of the possibility of a cumulative "feedback" process, whereby low productivity growth fuels its own decline. Low productivity growth holds down real incomes, while families quite naturally strive to protect their living standards at the supermarket and at the ballot box. They may achieve higher consumption both by reducing private saving and by rewarding politicians who promise to reduce taxes and increase public dissaving. This means even less investment for the future with a further weakening of productivity growth, and a repetition of this debilitating cycle.

We must act quickly and boldly as a society to interrupt this cycle, for the problem becomes harder to solve as its severity increases. **CED strongly believes that inadequate saving and investment, and correspondingly excessive consumption, is undermining our prospects for long-term economic growth, rising living standards, and international economic competitiveness and leadership. Meeting the fundamental economic goals of our society will be impossible if we cannot muster the political will to slow the growth of consumption and shift these resources to investment.** We must stop deluding ourselves into believing that continuing to live beyond our collective means is a formula for sustainable prosperity.

We require stronger public leadership than has been evident in recent years to educate the public about the economic consequences of inaction. Our political institutions dilute accountability. Our leaders have not successfully posed or resolved the hard choices involving sacrifice through temporary restraints in consumption growth.*

SUMMARY OF POLICY RECOMMENDATIONS: MOBILIZING RESOURCES FOR SAVING, INVESTMENT, AND GROWTH**

GETTING SERIOUS ABOUT NATIONAL SAVING AND DEFICIT REDUCTION

The long-term foundation of a national investment and growth strategy must be an increase in national saving.

- **Reversing the national saving collapse of the 1980s should become an explicit U.S.**

*See memorandum by JAMES Q. RIORDAN, (page 56).

**See memorandum by JAMES Q. RIORDAN, (page 56).

policy goal. We should aim to raise the rate of national saving in the next decade to its pre-1980 average of about 8 percent of national income.

The only certain policy to increase national saving is reduction of the large Federal budget deficits. Although the dire consequences of these deficits are staring us in the face, we have failed to make deficit reduction our top priority.

- **The main instrument for increasing saving must be deficit reduction. As an interim target, deficits should be reduced by an average increment of $50 billion each year for five years, so that in the fifth year the annual structural deficit is about $250 billion less than currently projected. This program should be phased in, and its *implementation* (but not its *enactment*) should depend upon the progress of economic recovery. To reach the national saving target, our ultimate goal should be a small surplus of about 1 percent of GDP in the total budget (including Social Security) within a decade.**

This is a large reduction, which will require painful and politically unpopular spending cuts in previously sacrosanct programs and almost certainly tax increases as well. However, it is not out of proportion to reductions made by other nations.

There have been many proposals to use tax incentives to increase *private* saving. However, such incentives normally increase the deficit and thus have an uncertain effect on total national saving. For this reason, we should be cautious in employing them, recognizing that other taxes, which may impose their own burden, may have to be raised to finance them.

- **While we believe that the most certain way to increase national saving is to reduce the Federal deficit, we support private saving incentives that can be shown to raise *national* saving or that are financed sufficiently to do so.**

REDUCING GOVERNMENT SPENDING

Any serious program of spending restraint must substantially reduce the growth of entitlement and transfer programs. These Federal expenditures have been the major source of budget growth, now consume well over half the budget, and go principally to high- and middle-income beneficiaries rather than the needy.

- **We applaud efforts to reduce the growth of entitlement spending. However, we urge that, where feasible, entitlement reductions be structured to minimize the impact on low-income beneficiaries.**

We must face up to the inescapable fact that such action must deal with Social Security and Medicare, which together represent almost 60 percent of entitlement spending. The real benefit levels in Social Security and Medicare are often regarded as sacrosanct, but their benefits must be weighed against their cost in reducing economic growth and the burden that they shift to future generations. In addition, while we do not recommend reductions in Medicaid benefit levels, liberalizations should not be extended until health care costs have been brought under control and state budgets have adjusted to recent changes.

- **As a matter both of equity and provision for national saving, we reaffirm CED's earlier recommendations that (A) Social Security benefits be taxed equivalently to private pensions; and that (B) the phase-in of the increase in the normal and early retirement ages be made more rapidly than current law provides. If Social Security payments are taxed like private pensions and the deficit has been brought under control, the earned income test for Social Security should be liberalized.**

The entitlement programs presenting the gravest threat to our fiscal future are the major health care programs. The "deficit problem" is rapidly becoming a "health care problem," and reduction in the growth of overall public and private health care costs must be part of any budgetary solution. Specific proposals for dealing with health care costs are beyond the scope of this statement.[7] Nevertheless, in view of the enormous budgetary implications of health care reform legislation:

- **No proposals for improving health care delivery should be actively considered**

unless they contain credible mechanisms for both controlling costs and fully financing any additional public expenditures.**

In addition to these very large entitlement programs, there are a number of other programs, such as some subsidies for agriculture and electrification, which no longer address the original problems for which they were created.

- **All entitlement programs should be carefully reviewed. They should be restructured to accord with their original purposes if they remain valid, or otherwise be terminated.**

In addition to entitlement restraint, discretionary spending for both defense and nondefense purposes must be cut back.

- **Defense expenditures should be reduced to the greatest extent consistent with our new national security requirements, and the resulting peace dividend should go to deficit reduction.**

The defense budget must not become a disguised jobs program. Domestic employment considerations are not an adequate rationale for rejection of even larger long-term military reductions than those now being planned. We recognize that the transition must be gradual and believe that adjustment policies should be enhanced if necessary to facilitate the largest possible reductions compatible with national security requirements.

Federal domestic discretionary spending for consumption or unproductive investment purposes should also be reduced. We believe the limitations on domestic discretionary spending set by the 1990 Budget Agreement have been useful and effective, although somewhat mechanical and compartmentalized.

- **New budget rules and procedures are likely to be adopted in 1993. We strongly urge that such rules continue to set enforceable limits on discretionary spending after giving full consideration to requirements for infrastructure, education, training, and other public investments. We also recommend that new budget procedures include some type of "enhanced** rescission" mechanism, whereby the Congress is obligated to vote on the President's rescission requests.

INCREASING REVENUES

CED strongly believes that deficit reduction should be achieved to the greatest extent possible through spending cuts. Yet, we recognize that the above spending cuts may be insufficient to reach our ambitious deficit reduction goals.

- **We reaffirm CED's view that carefully designed tax increases which do not discourage private saving and investment are less harmful to the long-term health of the economy than persistent structural budget deficits. If spending reductions sufficient to meet our budget targets cannot be enacted in spite of a vigorous attempt to do so, deficits should be reduced by raising additional revenues.**

Insofar as possible, any necessary tax increases should be designed to reduce consumption rather than saving and investment. In addition, since virtually all taxes impose an economic burden by distorting business and household decisions, tax increases should be designed to minimize such distortions.

- **To minimize economic distortions, tax increases should in general be levied on the broadest base possible to keep rates low. Any additional income tax revenues should be sought first in broadening the tax base by eliminating preferences, where such changes do not reduce national saving. In general, taxes on consumption should also be imposed on the broadest possible base. We also endorse the principle of additional taxes on the consumption of products which demonstrably impose external health, safety, and environmental costs which exceed current levels of taxation.**

INVESTING FOR GROWTH

Increasing saving — the resources available for investment — is only the first step. **These scarce resources must then flow efficiently into productive investments.** Freely operating capital markets normally allocate investment funds to their most productive uses.

However, tax and regulatory policies sometimes impede such efficient allocation.

Currently, our capital market tends to overallocate resources to housing investment due to generous tax subsidies. While America's residential housing is a great economic and social asset and the envy of other nations, we believe this bias goes too far at the expense of other investments which directly enhance productivity. We thus propose two measures to begin to "level the playing field."

- **CED recommends a tax credit on incremental equipment investments above a specified threshold, as is currently done in the research and experimentation tax credit.**

- **We also recommend a gradual reduction of the mortgage interest subsidy and that the subsidies for borrowing through home equity loans and the financing of second homes be phased out.***

It is widely recognized that economic growth depends upon investments in research and technology that often do not receive economically appropriate levels of private sector funding because the returns cannot be fully captured by private firms. We therefore also recommend that:

- **The research and experimentation tax credit be made permanent in order to stimulate adequate private sector research activities. Consideration should also be given to more rapid depreciation of R&D investments.**

- **Federal support for basic research should be increased, provided that strong principles of review are enforced and political earmarking of projects is curbed.**

- **Federal support for applied research to assist the commercialization of technological advances should be continued, provided that the process is protected from political intrusion and that the majority of financing is furnished by the private sector.**

The productivity of investment also depends upon the ability of business to plan ahead with reasonable certainty.

*See memorandum by JAMES A. JOHNSON, (page 57).

8

- **We strongly believe that the tax code should be made more stable. Effective tax legislation cannot be written in crisis-driven, closed-door "summit" meetings. Changes should be made less frequently and through a legislative process which allows for full public hearings and careful Congressional committee deliberation.**

Fiscal policy should not only remove barriers to efficient allocation of private-sector investment, but also employ more effectively the public resources it devotes to investment purposes. We believe that in the context of overall reductions in Federal spending, there should be an increasing emphasis on public expenditures which underpin long-term economic growth. However, **increases in public investment funding should be accompanied by measures which ensure that these investments are economically worthwhile rather than merely politically expedient.**

- **We recommend that grant formulas for the cost-sharing of infrastructure investments be adjusted to give state and local authorities a stronger incentive for rational investment decisions and that pricing mechanisms such as user fees be used more widely to ensure that the use of public capital is appropriately related to economic costs.**

CED has consistently emphasized the importance of *human capital* — the investments in people that unleash the productive potential of physical capital and technology — and has made numerous recommendations in the areas of education and training.[8] We will not repeat the specific recommendations in these areas in this statement. However,

- **We emphatically reaffirm the importance of human capital to our overall investment environment. Its quality will determine to a great extent whether global capital is invested here or abroad, and whether investments in the United States create highly productive, high paying jobs.**

We also wish to call attention to the importance of the overall policy environment, beyond budgetary policy, in attracting investment and raising productivity. Monetary, trade, competition, and regulatory policies must complement budget policy in supporting growth. Our relatively open, competitive, and unregulated markets have provided our economy with a flexibility which has enhanced our productivity. It will be essential, as we pursue higher productivity growth, that we maintain this flexibility by examining carefully the benefits and costs of changes in regulatory and other policies.

Finally, we emphasize that rational and responsible economic policies can contribute to enhanced prosperity only if there is public support for such policies. Stronger leadership by our policy makers must improve public understanding of the choices necessary for future prosperity and create the willingness of all Americans to share the pain of the adjustment equitably.

Chapter 2

American Economic Discomfort

For the last two years, the United States has been collectively apprehensive about its economic health. In July 1990, the economy turned down and entered a recession, thus ending a record eight years of uninterrupted peacetime growth. As payrolls were cut and output and incomes shrank, workers and employers alike began to feel the acute hardship that any recession brings with it.

Although aggregate comparison of economic downturns hides the many individual tragedies resulting from a job loss or business failure, it nevertheless reveals that the economy has experienced even leaner times in the not-so-distant past. In a historical context, the 1990-1991 recession was not especially deep. The total decline in output amounted to 2.2 percent, less than the 2.8 percent drop in 1981-1982 and far less than the 4.1 percent drop recorded in 1974-1975. Similarly, the unemployment rate climbed to an eight-year high of 7.8 percent, but this was well below the 9 to 10 percent rates experienced in the 1981-1982 and 1974-1975 recessions.

While the recession itself was less deep than almost all others since the end of World War II, the ensuing recovery has been the slowest on record by far — in fact, so slow that the term itself seems misplaced. Normal recoveries have been characterized by a period of rapid GDP growth (usually at an annual rate of 5 percent or more) as idle resources are brought into production. Yet, the current recovery has seen an annual GDP growth rate of only about 1.5 percent in its first five quarters. More important for workers, job creation has been lackluster. Based on history, by this period in the business cycle one would expect almost all lost jobs to have been replaced by

new ones. Yet, only about one-fifth of the more than two million jobs lost have been replaced thus far.

It is thus easy to see why the attention of the public and the media has been concentrated on our short-term problems, and we do not wish to belittle them. But we must not thereby lose sight of the more fundamental long-term problem of inadequate economic growth, which, as we note in Chapter 1, dwarfs the recession in its cost to the nation. It is to that problem that we now turn.

THE THREAT TO AMERICAN LIVING STANDARDS

Recent years have seen a threat to the heart of what America stands for: the ability to build and maintain a materially rewarding life by combining opportunity with hard work in a free and competitive society. The history and character of the United States have been very much defined by this economic opportunity, yet it is becoming increasingly elusive.

HOURLY WAGES AND COMPENSATION ARE STAGNATING

Over the last two decades, average real wages and compensation for American workers have stagnated. By comparison, average real wages more than doubled in the 25 years immediately following World War II. That rise in total and average earnings allowed vast numbers of families to move from a life with few amenities to one of comforts and even luxuries.

The sharp break that took place in the 1970s is shown in Table 1, which presents average rates of growth for two conventional measures of worker remuneration for the pre- and post-1973 periods.

Real compensation per hour for workers in the business sector is the broadest per-worker measure of hourly cash and noncash income (including employer contributions for health insurance, pension plans, and Social Security). A 1948-1973 average growth rate of 2.9 percent allowed it to more than double in the 25 years following the end of World War II. Since then, it has risen very slowly and is virtually unchanged today from its 1979 level. Average hourly wages of production and nonsupervisory workers are a more widely cited (but less comprehensive) measure of remuneration which shows an even more disturbing trend.[1] After real wages for this "blue collar" group registered almost uninterrupted annual gains averaging 2.2 percent through 1973, they began a slow but steady decline that continues today. By this measure, real wages are currently about the same as in the late 1960s.

Such aggregate data, of course, may conceal much that lies below their surface. Table 1 compares *average* wages and compensation for an entire, but changing labor force at different points in time. The average is affected by changes in composition of the labor force, and different sub-groups show very different pat-

terns. Most notably, average earnings for women have tended to rise in recent years, while those for men fell, and more highly educated workers of each sex fared far better than their less educated peers.[2]

The stagnation of average real wages also does not imply that the wages of a typical *individual* worker did not grow. Even if average wages in the aggregate are stagnant, an individual's earnings would normally rise over time as he or she gains skills, experience, and seniority. One therefore must follow the earnings profiles of particular *cohorts* of workers as they age to assess how representative earnings profiles have changed.

Figure 3 presents such average earnings profiles at ages 30, 40, and 50 for male full-time, full-year workers born about 1920 and 1940 and the position of a current worker of about 30, born in 1960.[3] There are two striking features. First, the earnings profile has become flatter; the earnings of younger individual workers have grown more slowly over time than those of their elders. Second, the "starting point" for younger workers, on average, has now dropped; even if today's younger workers experience significant earnings increases, they may *on average* do no better or little better than those born 20 years earlier. Indeed, for less educated young male workers, whose entry-level wages have dropped most severely, the chances are very high that their peak incomes will be significantly below those of their fathers.[4]

A final important point is that earnings have become more widely *dispersed* around the average; there is a growing gap between high and low earners. The growing dispersion appears to be related especially to changes in the nature of jobs, especially *within* occupations, that have increased the rewards for obtaining a good education and high skills, while also increasing the penalties for not doing so. Real earnings for workers with a high school education or less (who comprise over half the work force) have declined at about 2 percent per year since the early 1970s, while those of college graduates rose modestly.[5] These are, again, "snapshots" at different points of time rather than profiles of individual workers. However, growing inequality com-

Table 1

Select Measures of Worker Wages and Compensation, 1948-1989
Average annual rates of change, percent

	1948-73	1973-89
Real compensation per hour (a)	2.9	0.7
Average real hourly wages (b)	2.2	-0.4

(a) Includes wages and salaries and fringe benefits for payroll workers in *all* industries.

(b) Includes wages and salaries only for production and non-supervisory workers on nonagricultural payrolls.

NOTES: Data deflated by CPI-U-X1 price deflator after 1966; 1990-91 data omitted from calculation to avoid cyclical distortion.

SOURCE: U.S. Departments of Commerce and Labor

Figure 3

Average Real Earnings By Age Group
Male full-time year-round workers

Thousands of constant 1990 dollars

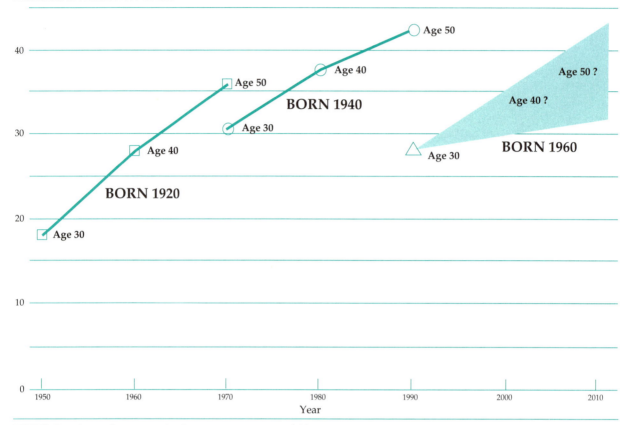

NOTES: Data for total compensation by age group is not available.
"Earnings" include only wages, salaries, and income from self-employment.
Earnings deflated by CPI-U-X1 after 1966.

SOURCE: U.S. Bureau of the Census

bined with a stagnant average means that an increasing proportion of *individual* workers and families will experience downward mobility — an actual drop in real incomes over time. For instance, roughly one-third of current male high school graduates may expect to earn less (in real terms) at age 40 than at age 30 if current trends continue.[6]

Of course, some wage and income variation is useful and expected in a well-functioning labor market where there are differences in employee skills, motivation, and other factors. Wage and income differentials are essential to a market economy in providing incentives for the hard work and risk-taking that are the bases of wealth creation. Never-

theless, there are both economic and political reasons why increasing dispersion of earnings and incomes may be undesirable, quite apart from subjective views of equity.

First, poverty may limit opportunity or otherwise prevent the development of human capital, which benefits society as a whole.[7] Second, political factors are also important. A systematic rupture of wage patterns among different groups in society, especially one that creates many "losers," may engender social and political conflict that is both harmful in itself and makes it harder to develop a sufficient majority for pro-growth economic policies. If a majority of the electorate believes that it has been left out while the fruits of growth have gone to others, it will exert pressure to distribute wealth more evenly. "Spreading the wealth" through redistributive policies is likely to stifle growth both by reducing incentives and by protecting inefficient activities. The danger that increasing income inequality will lead to policies which perpetuate low growth makes it vital that the United States raise long-term living standards for as many of its citizens as possible.

MORE WORK IS PROPPING UP INCOMES

Wages and hourly compensation, of course, tell only part of the story of living standards. A society can improve its material living standards by putting in more hours, and that is exactly what the United States has been doing for the last 20 years. Unlike hourly compensation, real income for the typical family has grown by over 10 percent, and by about 25 percent after adjustment for family size, over this period.[8]

Two concurrent demographic trends have increased the proportion of the total population in the labor force. First, the *size* of the working-age population relative to the total began to expand rapidly in the late 1960s and early 1970s, as the leading edge of the baby boom generation began entering the labor force. This pattern continued into the 1980s. Second, the *proportion* of working-age individuals who choose to be in the labor force, which held steady after World War II until the early 1970s, rose thereafter. Although work force participation rates have declined for men throughout the postwar era, this has been more than offset by increasing participation by women since about 1970. As a result, while income per worker barely changed, average household real income rose.

However, such income increases did not come without costs. "Income" as conventionally measured does not account for two important components of living standards, both of which have diminished as a result of more work effort. First, household services are genuine economic output, even though they are not statistically acknowledged as such. Second, leisure is usually a valued activity. Many of the new labor force entrants during the 1970s and 1980s were second earners who went to work to boost family incomes, while sacri-

ficing leisure and the product of household activities.

If employment-driven growth in incomes were to continue into the future, perhaps we would not have as much reason for concern. Unfortunately, such growth is not likely to continue. The demographic trends which have partly insulated (conventionally measured) family incomes from decline will eventually reverse. The labor force of tomorrow has already been born, and we know that it will be substantially smaller than that of the previous generation, absent accelerating immigration. As a consequence, labor force growth is projected to slow substantially in the next decade, with a corresponding decline in the labor force-population ratio. [9]

Added to this demographic change is a likely leveling off of labor participation rates for women. The participation rate for women has been growing more slowly in recent years and in fact stopped rising in 1991 for the first time in almost 30 years. This is due to two separate factors. First, labor force barriers for women have steadily broken down in the last two decades, allowing most women who want to (or must) work to do so. Second, the social and cultural shift that brought women into the labor force may have slowed, and more working women may now leave the work force in order to raise their families. Finally, the trend toward earlier retirement and shorter hours among male workers has continued, and there is no indication that it will reverse.

Thus, for the nation as a whole, it will become harder to shore up after-tax incomes by putting in more work. The outlook for income growth will become starkly bleaker beginning in about 2010, when the baby boom generation begins to retire. As today's large labor force becomes the large retiree contingent of tomorrow, each worker will have to feed, clothe, house, and otherwise support more elderly dependents. In effect, each 100 workers today support not only their own households' consumption but also that of 20 retired persons.[10] Beginning in about 2010, however, the number of retirees per 100 workers will swell until it reaches about 38 by 2030.[11] In addition, these retirees will tend to live longer, and their health care costs will be higher. All of these factors mean that workers must become more productive just to *maintain* incomes, much less increase them.

Such ominous projections underscore the critical need for stronger growth in real wages as the primary engine of household income growth. Improving and sustaining wage growth *now*, rather than waiting until the financial stress of large-scale retirement is imminent, can less painfully provide the resources for what otherwise may become an enormous problem. This sustained wage and income growth can only come from increased *labor productivity* growth.

Living standards in the sense of *private consumption expenditures* standards have risen faster than wages or incomes because the proportion of income consumed has risen to an all-time high, while saving and investment have fallen. This means that living standards are increasingly being maintained by borrowing from the future, by failing to grow our private capital rapidly enough, by running down our public infrastructure without maintaining and replacing it, and by making insufficient investments in education and technology.

PROVIDING FOR PUBLIC NEEDS

An apparently inevitable corollary of slow growth in incomes is a scarcity of public resources and a reluctance to address critical social needs. Strong income growth fosters a generosity of spirit that makes us more willing to commit resources to the public good. Conversely, citizens whose own incomes are squeezed by slow growth are reluctant to provide public resources at the cost of further reduction in disposable income. As social needs compete even more severely with private living standards for resources, an "us against them" attitude among sectors of society may arise, resulting in increased social tension and pressure to adopt shortsighted economic policies.

While public services are not conventionally included in measures of family income, their loss can substantially reduce real living standards. The deterioration of public safety in some urban areas is the most striking current example. Indeed, the public sector (in particular state and local governments) provides many vital services that are too often taken for granted, such as police and fire protection, sanitation, parks and recreation, and a host of other amenities that add to the overall quality of life. These public services should complement the private consumption derived from after-tax income. Today, however, the competition between the two for resources appears especially harsh. One can see this competition playing out in many fiscally strapped states, where the public has often been unwilling to accept tax increases even though very necessary public services are being significantly trimmed.

Even more important, other public expenditures, if efficiently managed, foster economic growth and development. As we shall see later, public investments in education, work force training, and infrastructure enhance productivity growth. A society that does not make needed public investments will ultimately have slower productivity growth, thereby squeezing incomes and further eroding the public's willingness to commit resources for public needs.

ERODING INTERNATIONAL COMPETITIVENESS AND LEADERSHIP

A second likely effect of domestic economic weakness is a reduced capacity to compete and lead internationally in the quest for prosperity and peace, whether privately in world markets or publicly in international political affairs.

A serious danger here is the erosion of global competitiveness in American industries, whether exporting or competing with foreign imports. A failure to compete successfully in international markets, including our own, is likely to unleash protectionist pressures which may cause us to turn our backs on a key engine of economic growth.

The expansion of international trade, assisted by U.S.-led efforts to lower trade barriers among nations throughout the post-World War II period, has been a principal factor in rapid world economic growth. U.S. economic strength and self-confidence allowed us to lead both developed and developing countries in demonstrating that liberal trade policies actually improve welfare in every country by furthering the process of product specialization, even though they may initially seem threatening. Every nation can be a winner in such a trading system, provided it regards open trade as a challenge to be met rather than a danger to be avoided.

During most of the post-World War II period, the benefits to the United States from open trade have been apparent. However, when the dollar was greatly overvalued during the early 1980s, a growing number of U.S. industries had trouble competing at home and abroad, and protectionist pressures rose sharply. Since then, the dollar has come down, improving U.S. price competitiveness in internationally traded goods and services. Nevertheless, this improvement in U.S. trade performance has been accompanied by stagnant real wages, which also raise protectionist pressures. Genuine competitiveness implies improved domestic living standards, as well as the ability to gain and hold markets.

In the public sphere, the danger is that our capacity to lead toward a more stable and prosperous world may be impaired. This may seem paradoxical in that only two years ago, the United States took the lead in forging a multilateral military alliance to repel Iraq's aggression against Kuwait. This, together with the sudden collapse of the Communist bloc in Eastern Europe and the ultimate demise of the Soviet Union, catapulted the United States to a position as the sole military superpower.

However, the fall of Communism has taught a second lesson: military strength can be supported over time only by a strong, competitive economy. A new era has begun in which economic strength will be the critical ingredient of world leadership. On this economic score, we believe that America is at a precarious crossroads. Although our military strength is unparalleled, economic weakness may divert us (and other nations) from initiating and supporting the broad global views of economic and political issues that have previously served us so well. Indeed, we are seeing strong pressures to "turn inward," and other countries appear less responsive to American initiatives and participation.

A related danger is that we may become increasingly reluctant to devote necessary resources to international security and economic development. Peacekeeping will remain expensive, even in a unipolar world, and calls for assistance are likely to grow. Rapidly developing economies can actually improve U.S. economic prospects by opening new markets, as recent experience in Mexico eloquently testifies.

A current example is provided by the disorganized economies of Eastern Europe and the former Soviet Union, which are struggling to restructure themselves for growth and stability. Although internal reform is the most important factor in these efforts, the evidence from German reunification suggests that significant external resources will be needed as well.

There are large potential benefits, especially the diminished likelihood of future conflict, from integrating these economies into a peaceful and prosperous world economic order. There are compelling economic reasons for the United States to join — and sometimes lead — other industrial democracies in providing transition resources where these would be productive. Such foreign aid should not be offered indiscriminately; indeed, many have criticized excessive foreign aid in the past as a form of international bribery. Yet, the United States seems more and more in danger of coming to the table in international discussions with empty pockets — not a posture enhancing world leadership and international security. The American public has become impatient with foreign commitments when domestic growth is weak, and this conflict will only increase as domestic living standards and resources become more tightly constrained.

Our economic problems have prompted many to suggest that American economic, political, and moral leadership in the world is declining due to practices of other nations, long-term historical forces, and other factors beyond our control. This Committee strongly disagrees with this assessment. The shortfalls and problems outlined above are substantially of our own making. **The stagnation of American living standards and the emerging threat to our international economic competitive-**

ness and leadership are primarily due to a substantial slowdown in the rate of productivity growth since the early 1970s. Unless this country is willing to take the necessary steps to raise productivity growth, these problems will continue to plague us, and our capacity to address them will progressively decline.

SLOW PRODUCTIVITY GROWTH IS THE FUNDAMENTAL PROBLEM

Although productivity growth rarely appears in front page economic headlines, it is quite simply the most important long-run determinant of a country's economic strength and living standards. It is far more important to our well-being than the Japanese trade barriers or European agricultural subsidies that dominate media discussion. In fact, the seemingly diverse and unrelated economic problems outlined above share a common thread — they all ultimately stem from lagging productivity growth.

Sustained productivity growth is the engine that has allowed the average American worker today to enjoy a standard of living unimaginable a century ago. In short, the growth of labor productivity is at the root of the unprecedented economic expansion which has characterized the nineteenth and twentieth centuries. To fully appreciate its importance, one must take a closer look at its impact on economic output.

Productivity growth by its nature affects the long-term development of wealth in a society rather than short-term fluctuations in production; indeed, that is why its importance as the foundation of economic growth is often misunderstood in short-term analysis. U.S. labor productivity growth has averaged just over 2 percent annually over the last hundred years. Such apparently small annual changes are nearly invisible as they pass. However, the power of compounding means that these small differences cumulate over decades to become huge differences in economic capacity and wealth. For example, if U.S. productivity growth over the past century had been at the 1980s average rate of 1 percent per year instead of 2 percent, our living standards would roughly match those of Thailand or Brazil.

Another way to demonstrate the importance of productivity growth is to examine its role in the evolution of a particular industry. Perhaps the most striking example of the changes productivity has brought to the modern world is in agriculture. A century ago, the United States was a predominantly agrarian nation, with fully half the labor force involved with food production. Even with this huge proportion of agricultural workers, lack of good transportation and refrigeration limited food supply to local goods, consisting mainly of low-quality foods such as potatoes, lard, cornmeal, and salt pork.

A little over a century later, the agrarian labor force has shrunk from half the total to under 3 percent of the work force; yet, it produces enough food for an abundant domestic supply plus substantial exports. In addition to this huge increase in quantity, the quality and variety of food have increased dramatically, as evidenced by any trip through a supermarket. The continual introduction of more productive and technologically advanced machinery has vastly improved the output of each farmer, freeing resources for other uses. Many other industries have undergone similar progressions from labor-intensive production at a subsistence level to improved capital-intensive production processes that have vastly increased consumer choice as well as national wealth through continuous productivity growth.[12]

While there are alternative measures of productivity (see "The Measurement of Productivity," opposite page), this discussion focuses on *labor productivity*. The primary purpose of this statement is to recommend policies to increase the capacity of the U.S. economy to *provide adequate economic resources for the future needs of society*, a capacity which is best gauged by labor productivity.[13]

Advances in labor productivity, coupled with changes in the number of workers and the hours they work, determine the rate of output growth. These concepts are normally applied to the *business sector*, which constitutes about 85 percent of total domestic output (GDP) and therefore fundamentally drives overall GDP growth. Table 2 shows how growth in productivity and work hours contributed to growth during the post-World War II period.

The table shows a striking shift in the two components of output growth. During the 1948-73 period, improvements in productivity (output per hour) accounted for 83 percent of

Table 2

Sources of Economic Growth, Business Sector

Average annual rates of change, percent

	1948-1973	1973-1989
Labor productivity growth	2.9	1.0
Plus: Growth in work hours	0.6	1.7
Equals: Business output growth	3.5	2.7

NOTE: 1990-1991 data omitted to avoid cyclical distortion.

SOURCE: U.S. Bureau of Labor Statistics

the growth in output, since hours worked increased at a very slow rate. Between 1973 and 1989, however, those proportions essentially reversed. Productivity growth fell by two-thirds, but the growth rate of hours worked tripled, offsetting much of the productivity decline. Thus, real output growth declined from an annual average of 3.5 percent between 1948-1973 to 2.7 percent between 1973-1989.

PRODUCTIVITY AND SUSTAINABLE GROWTH IN LIVING STANDARDS

The shift from productivity improvements to additional hours as a source of growth shown in Table 2 has profound consequences for *living standards*. Increases in output due to increased working hours obviously cannot raise real wages. Tax and transfer policies can redistribute this income to make some individuals richer and some poorer, but it is not possible for *average* wages to grow. If wages do not grow, the only way real family incomes can increase is if more people work, or people work longer hours, which entails the opportunity cost of leisure time and household activities. Increases in labor input are largely a function of demographic factors, and current trends indicate that future increases in work effort will be much smaller than in recent years. Thus, reliance on more work to sustain growth in living standards is not feasible over the long run.

Economic growth resulting from productivity growth, on the other hand, means increases in hourly wages and compensation. It is very easy to see why. Labor productivity is simply the ratio of total output to hours worked. About three-quarters of this output is returned to workers as wages and other compensation, so increases in labor productivity are invariably accompanied by corresponding gains in hourly compensation. Figure 4 illustrates this tight relationship.[14] Thus broad-based productivity gains mean that average incomes can increase without sacrificing leisure or household responsibilities, directly improving living standards (both material and nonmaterial) for the population as a whole.

The fundamental point is clear: while employment growth can increase the productive capacity of the economy as a whole, *only improvements in productivity can ensure a rising standard of living for a society over the long term.* The concern of most workers and families is not the size of GDP, but the size of their paychecks and purchasing power. They have good reason to worry. The productivity slowdown that began in the late 1960s has put downward pressure on many people's incomes which can no longer be offset by employment growth. If it is not reversed, income growth will continue to slow.

U.S. productivity growth is important in relation to that of other nations, as well as to our own expectations. Historically, lagging economic performance has been associated with a decline in international economic, political, and military influence as well as a drop in relative living standards. A useful example is provided by Great Britain. Over the past century, its output per worker increased sixfold, suggesting great economic progress. Yet, during this period, Britain fell from clear economic preeminence,[15] largely because output

Figure 4

U.S. Labor Productivity and Real Compensation Per Hour
1947-1991, scale 1982=100

NOTE: Compensation deflated by CPI-U-X1 after 1966.
SOURCE: U. S. Departments of Commerce and Labor.

per worker growth in other industrial nations was much higher. From a strict "internationalist" perspective, the arguments for American preeminence may not appear compelling. But that is not America's — nor any other nation's — perspective. For better or for worse, national pride is alive and well, both at home and abroad. It seems unlikely that Americans will happily slide into second-rate living standards in a world where others hold the reins of international leadership.

PRODUCTIVITY AND INTERNATIONAL COMPETITIVENESS

Productivity growth is also critical to a country's international competitiveness — its ability to profitably sell high quality goods at competitive prices, maintain its share of international markets, and balance its trade accounts, all while improving its own citizens' living standards.[16]

While a large trade deficit is often associated with a country's inability to compete in world markets, an export surplus does not necessarily imply that a nation is competitive in the above sense. Many countries with low productivity run export surpluses, and an advanced country with lagging productivity growth can normally maintain exports and limit imports by depreciating its currency. This reduces the price of exports, raises the cost of imports, reduces real wages and incomes, and (with appropriate macroeconomic policies) improves its trade balance. Many economically unsuccessful countries have used currency depreciation to balance their trade accounts while impoverishing their workers. Strong productivity growth is therefore important because it allows a country to remain competitive abroad *without* the costly effects of currency depreciation. Conversely, a country with high productivity may still run a large trade deficit if its currency is overvalued, as was true of the United States in the 1980s.

Genuine international competitiveness requires the successful combination of adequate productivity growth, which allows real wages to grow while costs remain low, with a realistic exchange rate and the managerial vision and marketing skills which can convert domestic success into foreign sales.

While productivity is a basic determinant of competitiveness, a loss of international competitiveness itself contributes to the productivity problem. A substantial source of productivity improvement appears to be related to cost reductions and improved returns on investment from economies of scale. Indeed, one reason the United States initially became so productive is that its large internal market provided ample economies of scale. Now even larger markets are opening up worldwide, offering new scale economies. If a country is not competitive in these markets, it will have difficulty reaping the productivity benefits of larger volumes.

THE DECLINE IN U.S. PRODUCTIVITY GROWTH

Considerable debate and confusion surround the contention that U.S. productivity growth has been "too slow" in recent years. Although this is partly a result of statistical disagreements over the measurement of productivity, it stems principally from uncertainty about what standard or goal should be used. No amount of research, of course, will yield a "correct" standard. Such goals derive from the importance that a society assigns to its future standard of living (both absolutely and in relation to that of other societies) and to its position and role in the world.

We believe that current U.S. productivity growth should be compared both with its own past performance, which determines the growth in wages and incomes we have come to expect, and with the performance of other leading industrial nations, which is the key determinant of long-term international competitiveness and leadership.

HISTORICAL TRENDS IN PRODUCTIVITY GROWTH

There is nearly universal agreement among researchers that the United States experienced a substantial productivity slowdown, beginning in the late 1960s, which accelerated sharply after 1973. Figure 5 amplifies the summary information displayed above in Table 2 by charting annual labor productivity growth

rates in the business sector since World War II. Productivity growth between 1973 and 1981 was particularly weak, averaging only one half of 1 percent per year, sharply below the 1948-1973 rate.[17] This growth rate was also well below that of other industrial nations. It is unclear what caused the slowdown, but researchers believe that inadequate investment in capital and R&D, inefficient and often excessive regulatory burdens, and an influx of relatively young and inexperienced workers into the labor force all played a part.[18]

There is somewhat more disagreement about whether the 1980s represented a continuation of the slowdown or a partial recovery. Productivity growth climbed substantially after the deep 1982 recession and remained at a respectable level for the next several years. However, Figure 5 indicates that productivity improvement from 1981 to 1991, averaging about 1 percent annually, was not enough to reverse the overall downward trend since 1973 and was nothing like the growth enjoyed in the 1950s and 1960s.

Figure 5

Growth in U.S. Output Per Hour Total Business Sector

Percent change from previous year

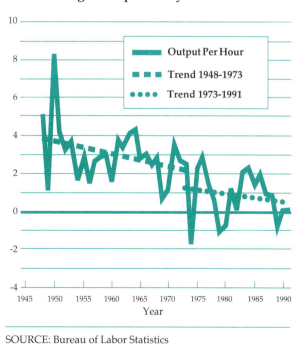

SOURCE: Bureau of Labor Statistics

Although *aggregate* productivity rates have continued to languish, the manufacturing sector has substantially rebounded from the slump of the 1970s. Figure 6 disaggregates productivity growth for manufacturing from the total business sector, and it clearly shows manufacturing did not contribute to the continuing productivity slowdown of the 1980s.

Such data must be read with care. A substantial portion of the numerical gain in manufacturing productivity resulted from layoffs caused by permanent shutdown of inefficient plants.[19] Obviously, layoffs can provide a one-time productivity boost but do not represent a source of *continuing* improvement. Furthermore, if these laid-off employees cannot find high productivity work in other non-manufacturing sectors, average productivity growth for the economy as a whole may even decline. From the point of view of competitiveness, the resurgence of manufacturing productivity is favorable. But productivity gains caused by a streamlined manufacturing sector cannot by themselves cure the productivity slowdown and accompanying wage stagnation. Living standards depend on the productivity of the *overall* economy. Since the manufacturing sector represents a shrinking proportion of total employment — now less than 20 percent of the labor force — it has become less important to raising the economy's overall productivity and living standards.

A critical corollary of this evidence is that some or all *private nonmanufacturing* sectors, which include transportation, trade, finance and insurance, and all other services, must be dragging down the average. These industries produce most of current U.S. economic output. If the productivity growth of these increasingly large sectors cannot be improved, it will not be possible for overall living standards to rise.

Some observers contend that the story told by official data from the post-World War II era is incorrect. A common criticism of these data is that they understate productivity growth, particularly in certain service industries, and that this downward bias has gotten worse in the last two decades. If this bias does exist, the shift of employment to the service sector that has occurred over the last several decades magnifies the bias.[20] By this analysis, we as a nation are much better off than we think we are with regard to productivity and living standards and have little reason to worry. Mismeasurement issues are certainly serious and extremely complex. However, most researchers believe that the *aggregate* productivity slowdown is much more real than imagined.[21]

Other scholars have recently suggested that the slowdown of the 1970s and 1980s does not necessarily mean that aggregate productivity growth is currently "too low" relative to longer-run historical standards. Although it is certainly lower relative to the earlier postwar years, examination of a longer period suggests that the "slowdown" reflects a return to a longer-run trend rate. This is only partly true. Figure 7 shows average annual productivity growth rates for periods beginning in 1889. The data reveal that the 1948-1973 period — with which the 1970s slowdown is conventionally compared — is well above historical rates. On the other hand, the "recovery" of productivity during the 1980s remains below not only the aberration of the postwar period but the century-long average of 2.1 percent as well.[22]

Figure 6

U.S. Output Per Hour Growth by Sector
Average annual percentage change

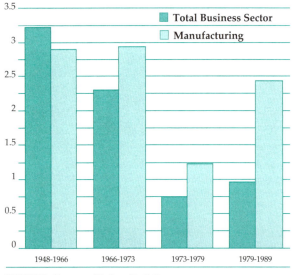

SOURCE: Bureau of Labor Statistics

INTERNATIONAL COMPARISONS OF PRODUCTIVITY GROWTH

In addition to suffering a productivity slow-down relative to its own past, the United States has recently had consistently lower productivity growth than nearly every country in the industrialized world. The top panel of Figure 8 shows average annual labor productivity growth for the Group of Seven industrial democracies.[23] It is interesting to note that the productivity slowdown was not limited to the United States; in fact, the slowdown was more pronounced in Japan. Even so, other countries still enjoy productivity growth that is about the same as the pre-slowdown rate in the United States.

Despite lower productivity *growth*, the United States still retains the highest absolute level of productivity of the major industrial nations, as shown in the bottom panel of Figure 8. The productivity levels of other economies were historically so much lower that even many years of their higher growth

Figure 7

Long-Term Trends In U.S. Output Per Hour Growth
1889-1989

Average annual percentage change

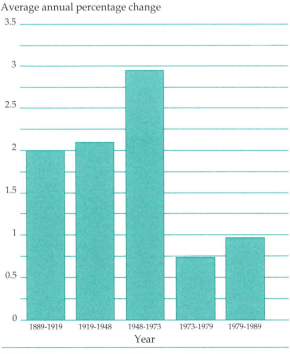

SOURCE: Kendrick (1991) and Bureau of Labor Statistics

Figure 8

Average Annual Percentage Change in GDP Per Worker, Selected Nations

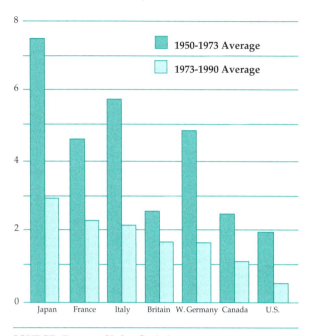

SOURCE: Bureau of Labor Statistics

International Comparison of Real GDP Per Worker, 1990
In 1990 U.S. dollars, converted using purchasing power parity ratios

Thousands

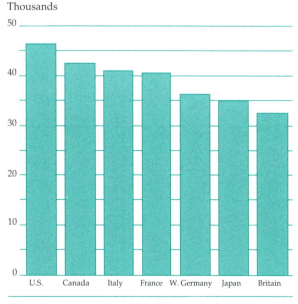

NOTE: Figures are adjusted for differences in local buying power.

SOURCE: Bureau of Labor Statistics

has not closed the gap.[24] It was noted earlier that growth in manufacturing productivity has been remarkably strong relative to the economy as a whole. In fact, the U.S. productivity growth rate in manufacturing has fallen less than in most other industrial nations, as Figure 9 shows. Recent estimates also indicate that American manufacturers remain the most productive in the world in absolute terms.[25]

Nevertheless, the clear implication of continued productivity growth differentials is that some other nations will eventually overtake and exceed U.S. productivity levels and living standards. Clearly, the once wide gap between the productivity of the American economy and that of our industrial competitors is fast narrowing. The key question is whether or not this trend will persist.

It is natural to speculate that different productivity levels among nations will converge on those of the leader. There are sensible theoretical arguments regarding technology transfer supporting this view, and the empirical evidence is also supportive. In general, the industrial nations that enjoyed the highest productivity growth rates in the years following World War II also experienced the largest slow-down during the 1970s and 1980s. If this trend continues, one would expect eventual convergence in productivity growth rates and levels. An even more compelling fact is that there is an almost perfectly inverse relationship between a country's productivity *level* at the end of World War II and its average annual productivity *growth rate* during the postwar period. Such data suggest that the United States may be "right on schedule" with respect to productivity growth, and possibly even above where it historically and statistically "should be."[26]

However, this model of convergence can become too mechanistic if allowance is not made for the effects of public policy on economic performance and productivity growth. A nation is not preordained to live with whatever productivity growth is statistically allotted to it as a result of its current productivity level in relation to that of others. In fact, both growth accounting studies and the voluminous research conducted in response to the 1970s productivity slowdown in the United States indicate that productivity growth, while imperfectly understood, can be affected by investments in certain factors of production, the amount of which can be influenced by public policy decisions.[27]

Regardless of whether measured by historical or international standards, current overall productivity growth is too low to meet our long-term domestic and international economic needs. We have already noted that the reduction in the labor force-population ratio which is certain to result as the large baby boom population retires beginning around 2010 will put downward pressure on living standards. If these trends are not offset by stronger productivity growth, living standards of workers and retirees will be squeezed, resulting in corrosive social and political conflicts. **We are obligated to try to avert such conflicts by restoring higher productivity growth.** However, it should *not* be assumed that a trend rate, regardless of the period it spans, is a reliable forecast of future productivity. Productivity growth is not handed to us on a silver platter. It is a function of how our society chooses to use (or misuse) its economic resources. As we shall see in Chapter 3,

Figure 9

Labor Productivity Growth in Manufacturing, Selected Nations
Average annual percentage change

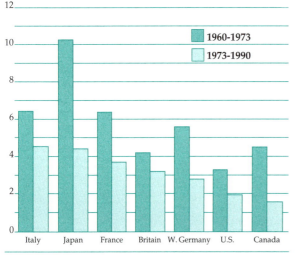

1960-1973
1973-1990

Italy Japan France Britain W. Germany U.S. Canada

SOURCE: Bureau of Labor Statistics

many policy decisions of recent years have been severely biased *against* productivity growth. Correction of these decisions can boost productivity growth above its trend, which should be our top long-term economic priority.

INCREASED INVESTMENT: THE SOURCE OF PRODUCTIVITY GROWTH

To raise productivity growth, the United States must raise both private and public investment. By "investment" we mean something much broader than traditional concepts of factories and machines. We define investment as the commitment of resources to activities which raise future output rather than to current consumption — the production of "seed corn" rather than bread. In practice, investment may encompass a "triad" of interdependent activities that increase the stock of physical, technological, and human capital. The technological and human capital components must be considered as very broad concepts; they encompass, for instance, a broad array of management and organizational skills which may not lend themselves to mechanistic or even quantitative interpretation.

New investment in physical capital is a key element of sustained productivity growth. At an intuitive level this is obvious; adding modern capital equipment can enhance worker productivity. The empirical evidence is quite strong. Statistical studies of the post-World War II era indicate that a 1 percent increase in the capital-labor ratio is associated with at least one-third of 1 percent (and possibly more) of additional productivity growth, an exceedingly tight correlation.[28] Of course, this association by itself does not indicate whether investment in physical capital causes growth or vice versa. However, recent research strongly suggests that the direction of causation runs primarily from investment (particularly investment in machinery and equipment) to growth. In addition, this research suggests that equipment investment may generate returns to society of 20 percent or more, significantly above the private returns to investors assumed in traditional growth accounting.[29]

There are other types of physical investments which, although less directly related to the production process than machinery and plant, nonetheless are key ingredients in productivity growth. The most important are the transportation, communications, and sanitation networks loosely referred to as "infrastructure." Intuition and economic history attest strongly to the importance of infrastructure — witness the opening of the American West. Current events in Eastern Europe also speak eloquently; a staggering amount of Russian harvested agricultural goods rot in the fields for lack of adequate transportation capacity. Clearly, an economy with state-of-the-art production facilities will be much less productive without a complementary infrastructure.

However, quantifying the contribution of infrastructure to productivity growth is a matter of considerable controversy. Several studies have purported to show very large returns from infrastructure investment, but they have been widely criticized.[30] But, the assertion that infrastructure has little or no effect on productivity growth is also implausible. Whether or not existing infrastructure adequately supports the private capital stock will be taken up in Chapter 3.

Investments in science and technology to improve the effectiveness of machines, people, and other factors make extremely large contributions to productivity growth. Research on economic growth suggests that only about one-quarter to one-half of increases in labor productivity can be explained by increases in the physical capital stock. Some of the remainder has been due to structural changes in the economy and other factors, but most is related to "intellectual inputs" such as education and technology. Studies over the last several decades have consistently shown high private returns and even higher returns to society as a whole from private R&D expenditures.[31] Thus, enlarging the capital stock is only part of the growth equation; it must be continually nourished by cutting-edge innovations.

Physical and technological capital work together in a symbiotic relationship to assure that a country's labor force has access to a large and highly sophisticated capital stock.

However, the mere existence of such a capital stock will not boost productivity by itself. That potential has to be unlocked by workers. **The ability of the labor force to take advantage of the capital stock and technology at its disposal is a critical link between investment and growth**. This ability is very much dependent on education, training, and effective management. In a world where capital equipment, raw materials, and technology are crossing borders ever more freely, a country's productive edge will increasingly hinge on investments in "human capital" — education, training, and management skills that attract global capital and allow managers and workers to make the most of new technologies. One respected estimate suggests that about 30 percent of the increase in U.S. labor productivity from 1929 to 1982 was due to increased educational attainment.[32] In addition to this direct contribution of human capital to productivity, contributions are made by experimentation, motivation systems, and the well-recognized "movements up the learning curve." Much recent research confirms that the "human factor" has a substantial effect on the degree to which traditional investments in physical and technological capital are able to increase productivity.

It should be clear that increased productivity is essential to providing real solutions to the nagging doubts about America's future. Because the precise relative contributions of additional physical, technological, and human capital to productivity growth are not well understood, we believe that the most sensible strategy is a broad and balanced spectrum of investments in plant and equipment, selected infrastructure, technology, and human capital. Yet, our collective economic and political behavior, both private and public, has paid little heed to these requirements. As the next chapter shows, our commitment to investments in the future has been painfully inadequate.

Chapter 3

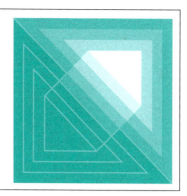

Overconsumption, Underinvestment, and the Federal Budget

PRESENT VERSUS FUTURE: THE NATION'S FUNDAMENTAL CHOICE

Every society faces a fundamental choice about how much of its product it should enjoy today as consumption and how much it should invest to provide for the future. The United States, despite its long history of economic growth and high living standards, is no exception. All societies face a basic resource constraint: Production can be used for today's consumption or investment for tomorrow's, but not for both. More investment means lower consumption and stronger growth today, but higher consumption tomorrow.

This allocation of the nation's resources between consumption and investment is principally determined by *saving*, which is the result of both private and public decisions. Private individuals and households decide how much of their current income to save rather than consume. Private businesses decide how much of their earnings to retain and reinvest rather than pay out as dividends. Governments decide how much to spend and tax, with public surpluses augmenting and deficits diminishing the saving done in the private sector.

The basic choice is illustrated in Figure 10.

Figure 10

Real Consumption Per Capita Under Two Saving and Investment Scenarios

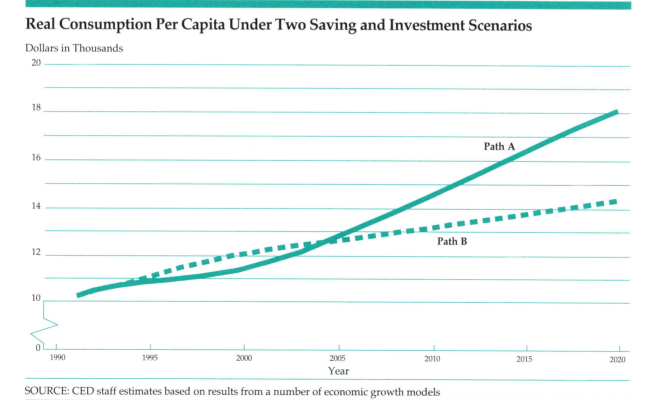

Dollars in Thousands

SOURCE: CED staff estimates based on results from a number of economic growth models

Path A represents consumption per person in a U.S. society that chooses in 1993 to save and invest for future prosperity. After a temporary slowing of consumption growth, it reaps the benefits of higher productivity and higher future consumption. Path B depicts a U.S. society that decides to "muddle through" large budget deficits and relatively low saving and investment. Although this society enjoys more rapid consumption growth for a period of years, the cost in terms of lost future consumption is large, quite apart from the loss of additional resources for public purposes.

THE UNITED STATES IS OVERCONSUMING AND UNDERINVESTING

In comparison with its own history and with many other advanced countries, the United States is making the consumption and saving decisions illustrated by Path B in Figure 10. There has been a dramatic shift in the use of economic resources for consumption rather than investment stretching back over several decades. As shown in Figure 11, personal consumption expenditures are now at a post-World War II high of about 75 percent of net domestic product (NDP), up from an average which fluctuated around 70 percent prior to the early 1970s. In effect, our society has decided to consume about 5 percent more of its net output each year than it did a few years ago. The national shift toward consumption took its toll on net private domestic investment, which fell by roughly 3 to 4 percent of NDP relative to the earlier postwar period. Investment would have fallen even more had the United States not borrowed capital from abroad for those investments for which we had insufficient saving. (This borrowing, however, has substantial costs.) The United States is in effect "eating its seed corn" — that is, reducing tomorrow's harvest for today's consumption.[1]

Net investment in the United States is also low by international standards. As the first panel of Figure 12 shows, net domestic investment in the United States has hovered around 3 to 5 percent of NDP in the last several years and is on the decline. The second panel of the chart shows a similar trend for net national

saving, but the U.S. rate is even lower, currently about 2 percent of NDP. Both measures are far below comparable rates for our largest industrial competitors, Japan and Germany.

What explains the apparent shortfall of American investments in new machinery, factories, and innovation? Some argue that excessive speculation in financial markets has forced investment managers to adopt short-sighted strategies which result in poor investment decisions. A detailed analysis of this subject is beyond the scope of this statement. However, it is closely related to a second and more fundamental explanation. Real long-term interest rates have been unprecedentedly high in recent years, raising the cost of capital to American firms and creating strong incentives for managers to shorten their time horizons. And these high real interest rates are related to the decline in U.S. national saving.

Figure 11

Private Consumption and Net Private Domestic Investment
As a percentage of net domestic product

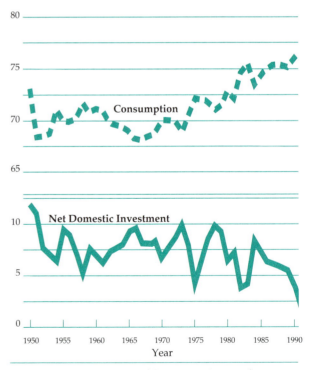

SOURCE: U.S. Department of Commerce, Bureau of Economic Analysis

Figure 12

International Comparison of Net Domestic Investment
As a percentage of net domestic product

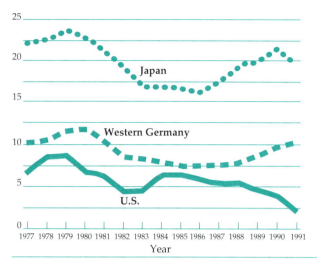

International Comparison of Net National Saving
As a percentage of net domestic product

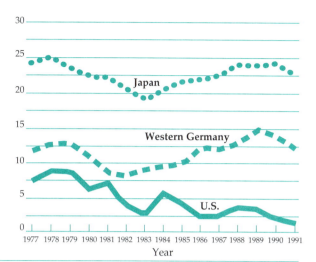

NOTE: 1991 value for Japan based on annualized first quarter data.
SOURCE: Organization for Economic Cooperation and Development

INCREASED INVESTMENT REQUIRES HIGHER NATIONAL SAVING

Over the long term, increases in the supply of investable funds must ultimately come from higher national saving. Of course, investment need not be constrained by domestic saving in any single year; the increasing integration of world financial markets has made it easier for countries to borrow financial resources from abroad to supplement domestic saving. Such foreign borrowing may allow nations to invest for development, as the United States did in the nineteenth century, or to consume more than they produce and "live beyond their means." In recent years, the United States has done the latter — borrowing abroad in unprecedented amounts in order to have its cake and eat it too. Figure 13 shows how the United States, which ran small trade and current account surpluses through most of the postwar period, went deeply into debt in order to avoid the difficult choice between reducing consumption and domestic investment in the 1980s.

The strategy of borrowing abroad to avoid difficult choices is likely to be unsustainable

Figure 13

U.S. Current Account Balance and Net International Investment Position
As a percentage of GDP

NOTE: Net foreign investment position equals total value of U.S. assets abroad less value of foreign assets in U.S.
Net investment position reflects direct investment valued at current cost. Comparable data not available before 1976.

SOURCE: U.S. Department of Commerce, Bureau of Economic Analysis

27

over the long term, and may well become problematic even in the short term. As any family knows, borrowing must eventually be repaid or refinanced, so the problem is merely postponed, not eliminated. In addition, borrowing entails servicing costs. Our foreign creditors actually or effectively own the additional productive capital invested in the United States. The dividends and interest from this capital are paid abroad and reduce American incomes just as lower domestic investment would, though not necessarily to the same extent. Finally, running the large trade deficits necessarily entailed by borrowing, and selling U.S. fixed domestic assets to finance them, may create political tensions which encourage protectionist policies and ultimately damage U.S. global competitiveness. [2]

If we cannot borrow from abroad indefinitely, U.S. domestic investment eventually will have to be financed by our own saving. Saving is done by households, businesses, and governments at the Federal, state, and local levels. The total of this saving, after allowing for that required to finance the replacement of depreciating capital, is *national saving*. As shown in Figure 14, national saving has declined very sharply in recent years. This is a result of a number of developments in both the private and public sectors:

- *Personal saving by households* has fallen very substantially in the last decade, as Figure 15 shows. Though it is common for the personal saving rate to fluctuate from year to year, the precipitous drop during the mid-1980s was unprecedented. The reasons for this are not well understood, although it appears to result from both economic and "psychological" factors.[3] The low average personal saving rates since 1980 account for about 1 percentage point of the total drop in national saving relative to the 1950-1979 period, or about 20 percent of the total decline.

- *Corporate saving* was also down in the 1980s. Although the *gross* corporate saving rate has been fairly stable, a large portion of this saving is used to replace and modernize retired and obsolete plant and equipment. As depreciation rates have increased,

reflecting shorter-lived capital, the *net* addition to the capital stock provided by corporate saving appears to have declined from 3 percent of GDP on average before 1980 to about 1.8 percent of GDP in the late 1980s.

- *Saving by state and local governments*, which was inconsequential in aggregate in the 1950s and 1960s, rose substantially in the 1970s as requirements for the funding of state and local government pension plans changed. The state and local government surpluses, which rose to nearly 1.5 percent of GDP in 1984, have recently fallen sharply as state and local operating budgets have gone dramatically into deficit. This appears to have been due both to a rising spending trajectory during the 1980s, for which continued financing would have been difficult in any case, plus a substantial shortfall in revenues during the prolonged recession of 1990-1991. However, these unfavorable fiscal developments have been offset to

Figure 14

U.S. Net National Saving
As a percentage of net domestic product

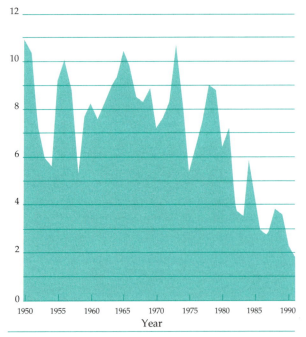

SOURCE: U.S. Department of Commerce, Bureau of Economic Analysis

Figure 15

U.S. Personal Saving Rate
As a percentage of disposable income

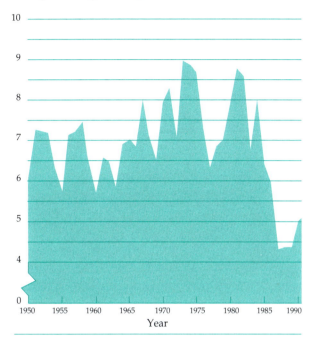

SOURCE: U.S. Department of Commerce, Bureau of Economic Analysis

some degree by state pension funds, which continue to grow. Thus, in the aggregate, state and local governments actually increased their savings rates on the average from 1980 to 1991.

• Finally, and most important, the *Federal budget deficit* increased significantly during the 1970s and then rose even more dramatically during the 1980s, producing an unprecedented increase in government *dissaving* and thereby a reduction in national saving.

The combined result of these factors was a collapse in U.S. national saving during the 1980s. Whereas national saving had run 8 to 9 percent of national income between 1950 and 1980, it fell to approximately 3 percent during the 1980s and declined to closer to 2 percent at the end of the decade and in 1990-1991.

THE IMPACT OF LOW SAVING ON PRODUCTIVITY GROWTH

Low saving rates hurt productivity growth by raising real interest rates and depressing spending on productive investments in physical, technological, and human capital. We appear to be moving in just this direction. The high cost of our recent and relatively sudden shift to a low-saving economy is suggested by a recent estimate that the decline in national saving during the 1980s had by 1990 reduced U.S. capital stock growth by at least 15 percent. This gradual erosion has reduced potential GDP by about 5 percent below levels consistent with the pre-1980 saving rates, and these losses could double by the end of the decade.[4] In dollar terms, the cost of our lower national saving during the 1980s now amounts to close to $300 billion per year in foregone output, and this cost will only increase if nothing is done to reverse the excessive growth of consumption in recent years.

While the current national saving rate may be somewhat depressed as a result of a very weak economy, it does not appear that the nation is currently prepared to save more than roughly 2 to 3 percent of its national income. There is considerable uncertainty about the size of the impact of investment and growing foreign debt on economic growth, but estimates suggest that a national saving rate of 5 to 5.5 percent would be required simply to maintain our currently low annual productivity growth rate of about 1 percent.[5] In fact, we will need more saving than that. The coming retirement of the baby boom generation and slowing labor force growth will put significant downward pressure on living standards which cannot be fully offset by current productivity growth.

While the above analysis shows the significant long-term cost of our high consumption and low saving relative to other countries and to our own recent history, it remains legitimate to ask, "What is the problem?" After all, what *is* the "right" tradeoff between present day consumption and saving for the future? Families and businesses presumably make consumption, saving, and investment choices in free markets that reflect their preferences, and public preferences are freely expressed at the ballot box. Apart from chauvinistic concerns about being "Number One" in the economic growth league, are there reasons to believe that market forces do not have it right and that the saving decisions made by individuals and policy makers in the public sphere do not produce the appropriate amount of saving?

To some extent, the appropriate amount of national saving undoubtedly is a social and political judgment rather than the result of individual economic preferences. For example, views will differ on how affluent our collective grandchildren should be at the expense of living standards today, or on America's appropriate future role and influence in the world and the resources required to secure it. However, there are also reasons why society may save too little, even in the relatively narrow terms of individual economic choice.

- Most of us would consider a society to be composed of several generations, not simply those adult individuals living, saving, and voting today. Future generations should be represented in decisions about their welfare in some way, but it is doubtful that either market or political processes perform that function adequately.[6]

- Individuals and businesses may save and invest too little under circumstances in which they cannot capture all of the returns to a given investment. A classic example is investment in research and development.[7] Such investments have what economists call "externalities," meaning that they have social benefits which are greater than the economic rate of return for any given firm making the investment. In such cases, investments with low private returns will not be made even though they are profitable for society as a whole.

- Institutional arrangements, such as unfunded Social Security pensions, may reduce the incentive for individual saving below that required to generate the income growth required to finance the pensions.

- Last, but certainly not least in current circumstances, there is substantial doubt that the large Federal budget deficits reflect informed political judgments about the appropriate amount of national saving. This may indicate poor public understanding of the long-term consequences of inadequate saving. However, it also reflects a common "collective choice" problem: The natural political efforts of different interest groups to protect their shares of public consumption (budget expenditures) produces a *collective* saving total which is lower than any group would prefer.

For all of these reasons, there is a reasonable rationale for public policy to be concerned with the rates of saving, investment, and economic growth. We believe that the nation's rate of saving and investment is too low to provide adequately for the future in terms of private living standards, likely public needs, and America's international economic and political role.

MUCH OF THE SAVING-INVESTMENT DECLINE IS DUE TO PUBLIC POLICY

Changes in Federal budget policy in recent years have played a significant role in the collapse of national saving and net investment. This has taken place in three principal areas: fiscal policy, the structure of taxes, and changes in the composition of Federal expenditures.

The most important and conspicuous public policy failure has been the sharp increase in public dissaving produced by the large and chronic Federal budget deficits. As shown in the top panel of Figure 16, total revenues have risen only slightly as a share of GDP during the postwar period, generally fluctuating within the range of 17 to 19 percent. Federal spending, however, has risen steadily, averaging 18 percent of GDP in the 1950s, 19 percent in the 1960s, 20.5 percent in the 1970s, and jumping sharply to 23.2 percent from 1980 to 1991.[8] (In spite of the rhetorical attention given to fiscal restraint during the 1980s, Federal spending was a larger share of GNP in *every year* during the 1980-1991 period than in *any* other prior postwar year.) As a result, the Federal deficit rose from an average of about 0.6 percent of GDP in 1950-1969 to 2.1 percent in the 1970s and 4.1 percent in the 1980s. In 1991 to 1992, it will be in the range of 5 to 6 percent of GDP, reflecting the very large (but hopefully temporary) costs of deposit insurance, lower revenues due to the 1990-1991 recession, and recent unfavorable reestimates of revenue collections and Medicaid costs.

CED has recognized for many years that fiscal policy should be based on the "structural," or high-employment, deficit rather than the actual deficit, which is affected by the short-term condition of the economy, not just the stance of fiscal policy. The lower panel of Figure 16 shows the structural deficit during the postwar period. It shows the large degree to which the huge deficits in recent years have been a result not of a weak economy, but of a structural gap between expenditures and revenues stemming from inappropriate policies. The structural deficit shows the same postwar increasing trend as the actual deficit, with a very sharp increase during the 1980s.

The immediate cause of the sharp increase in the structural deficit in the early 1980s was

Figure 16

Federal Spending, Revenues, and Deficits
As a percentage of GDP

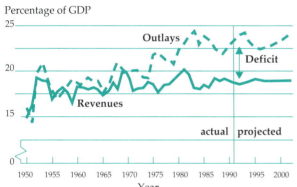

SOURCE: Congressional Budget Office and Office of Management and Budget

Structural Deficit as a Percentage of Potential GDP
1956-1992

Percentage of potential GDP

SOURCE: Congressional Budget Office

the government's decision in 1981 to reduce taxes and accelerate the defense buildup begun in the late 1970s without cutting domestic expenditures commensurately. This policy-related deficit then produced a large increase in debt service costs, and a cumulative process ensued in which larger deficits fed the accumulation of debt, which in turn gave rise to larger interest costs and still larger deficits. This large overhang of interest costs has now become exceedingly important to the total deficit outlook. The budget agreement of 1990, in addition to the policy measures taken at various times during the late 1980s, reversed much of the increased gap between spending and revenues related to *government policies*, as distinct from debt-service costs. The greatly increased burden of debt service continues, however, as a legacy and reminder of our earlier policy mistakes.

Figure 17 shows how the growth of the Federal budget deficit contributed to the overall decline in national saving. Nonfederal saving — the combined saving of households, business, and state and local governments — averaged 9 percent of national income before 1980, but declined to under 7 percent at the end of the 1980s. At the same time that nonfederal saving was falling, the Federal deficit rose rapidly, with the result that Federal borrowing now absorbs nearly two-thirds of nonfederal saving, compared with 20 percent in the 1970s and a negligible proportion in the 1950s and 1960s. In effect, the Federal deficit has drained larger and larger amounts from a shrinking pool of saving, leaving sharply diminished resources for the nation's future.

Some analysts subscribe to the view that deficits actually have negligible effects on national saving due to a phenomenon called "Ricardian equivalence." According to this notion, households and firms realize that the Federal deficit will eventually have to be repaid by the public in the form of higher taxes or lower spending, so they anticipate these policy changes by saving more of their own income to offset the deficit. While this view is theoretically plausible, it is not supported by the record. Indeed, the 1980s represented a crude test of the hypothesis. Deficits grew enormously, but, as Figure 17 shows, far from compensating for high deficits, nonfederal saving *fell* substantially, with a resulting collapse in net national saving.

CED has repeatedly warned that continued structural deficits would raise real interest rates and depress investment, inevitably eroding long-term economic growth and living standards. It has sometimes appeared that this price would be paid, if at all, only in some future "long term," perhaps by another generation of Americans. While those future costs will be great, we believe that the long term has arrived for us today. We have seen larger deficits crowd out productive investment and balloon our foreign debt during the 1980s. Now the costs of those deficits have reached society at large by robbing workers of potential wage increases and reducing the ability of governments to carry out public services.

In addition to raising the structural deficit, **Federal budget policy has discouraged saving and productivity-enhancing investment**

by subsidizing current consumption and investments in housing through the tax code. Prior to 1986, consumer interest was fully deductible, as were state and local sales taxes. The phasing out or elimination of these provisions in the 1986 law was a major step in reducing subsidies for consumption. However, one hand giveth what the other taketh away. Another provision of the 1986 Act allowed for the deductibility of interest on home equity loans, which while most often tapped for home improvement funds and repayment of other debts, in fact can be used — and indeed are widely advertised — as tax deductible instruments for financing consumption.[9]

More important, the tax system provides a major incentive for the diversion of resources to residential housing from other investments by allowing home buyers to exempt mortgage interest payments from tax.[10] The social return on investment in housing is estimated to be

Figure 17

Federal Deficits and National Saving
As a percentage of net domestic product

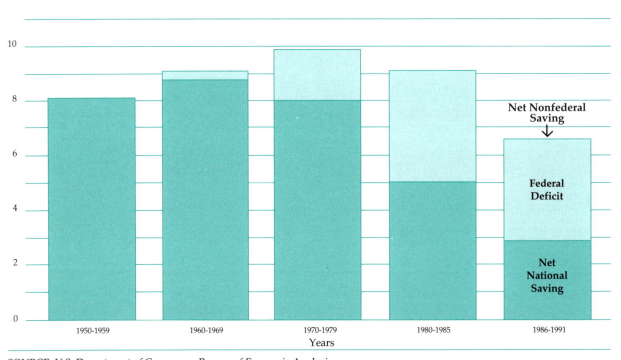

SOURCE: U.S. Department of Commerce, Bureau of Economic Analysis

only about half of the equivalent return on other investments, suggesting a gross misallocation of capital. Although part of this gap may be a natural reflection of the perceived riskiness of investments, it appears that roughly half of the costly distortion is due to the tax code.[11]

Home ownership is a justifiably valued part of American culture, and we as a country can take pride in a housing stock of unmatched quality and comfort. Indeed, for many people, their home is the only investment they own and was regarded as a hedge against high inflation in the 1970s. Thus, there may be social reasons unrelated to the economically efficient allocation of capital for encouraging home ownership. Nevertheless, the current subsidy for housing investment misallocates capital and thereby reduces future American wages and incomes. The paradox here is that the mortgage interest deduction is capitalized into the value of the house. This tends to inflate home prices, which is counter to the goal of the deduction itself. The effective result is that many individual home owners do not substantially benefit from the subsidy, even though the economic costs to society from the misallocated capital are large.

Finally, although the 1986 Act probably substantially reduced the distortions of incentives for investment among industries, the disincentive for saving and investment *as a whole* apparently increased as a result of a large shift of tax burdens from labor income to capital income. The higher rate of tax on capital income also tends to drive investment abroad. Thus, there still remains a substantial tax bias against productivity-enhancing investment as a result of the subsidy for residential housing and the relatively high effective tax rate on income from capital, especially in the noncorporate sector.[12]

Changes in the composition of Federal expenditures have encouraged private consumption and reduced public investments. The most conspicuous shift in spending priorities has been the rapid expansion of transfer payments in entitlement programs. This shift in the structure of the budget has been quite remarkable. Federal transfer payments were less than half of Federal pur-

chases of goods and services in 1960, but are now about 20 percent larger than direct purchases and indeed represent half of all Federal spending. The function of these payments is to supplement private disposable income, the vast majority of which is consumed. Furthermore, these transfers now go predominantly to middle- and high-income rather than poor beneficiaries. (However, the expansion of Social Security and Medicare in the 1960s and 1970s was a major factor in reducing poverty among the elderly, and there remains a substantial concentration of elderly with incomes not far above the poverty line.) Only 19 percent of Federal transfer payments are currently based on income tests, and only 27 percent of the families receiving cash transfers in 1990 had incomes below $15,000. Contrary to popular perception, "welfare costs" are not a large share of the Federal budget, but tax and transfer payments between different generations of the middle class certainly are a large and ever-growing share.[13]

In addition to encouraging private consumption, Federal spending priorities have moved away from productive public investments. The above discussion of national saving assumes that all investment takes place in the private sector, and indeed that is the conventional way the United States constructs its national income accounts. However, Federal purchases of goods and services which produce future income and services (and grants to state and local governments for such purchases) are in fact saving and investment, not consumption. Just as additional plant, equipment, technological know-how, and training in the private sector raise the productivity of labor, so do infrastructure, education, and research and development in the public sector when appropriate investment decisions are made. Had the sharply increased deficits of the 1980s been due to rising public investments of this kind, they would have done less damage and the outlook for economic growth would be much brighter today.

Unfortunately this was not the case. As shown in Figure 18, Federal nondefense spending on investment-type activities fell dramatically in the early 1980s and did not recover.[14] Even more striking is the longer-term trend. In l962, Federal outlays for long-term investments were about 20 percent of total nondefense outlays. However, the ensuing expansion of consumption-oriented programs vastly reduced the relative importance of investment, effectively halving its share of total nondefense outlays to 10 percent.

Many Federal long-term investments contribute to the "triad" of investments in physical, technological, and human capital outlined in Chapter 2. However, public investment, unlike private investment, is determined by a political process not subject to market tests, and its later benefits similarly are not usually governed by prices or other mechanisms to promote efficient use and maintenance. Therefore, major questions arise about the economic returns from such investments.

As explained in Chapter 2, Federal investments in "core infrastructure" — highways, airports, sanitation facilities, and power generation equipment — contribute to economic development and productivity. Though there are serious disagreements about the returns on incremental investments, there is universal agreement that a quality infrastructure is necessary to support and complement private activities. Figure 19 shows the ratio of the stock of "core infrastructure" to the private nonresidential capital stock over the postwar period,

Figure 18

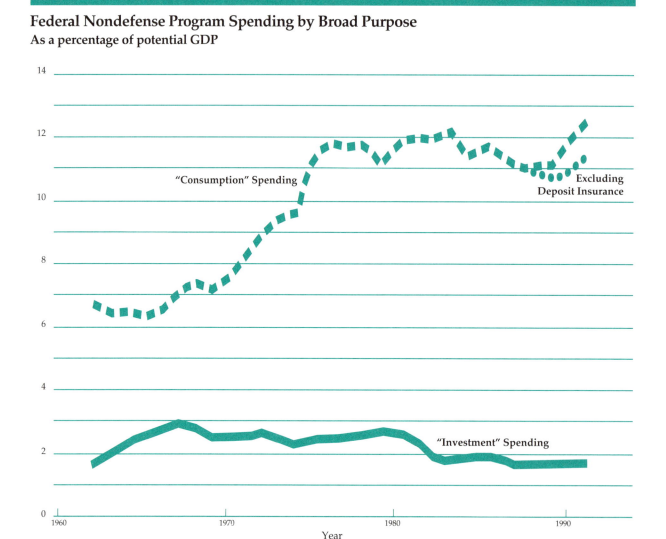

Federal Nondefense Program Spending by Broad Purpose
As a percentage of potential GDP

SOURCE: Office of Management and Budget

34

Figure 19

Core Public Infrastructure
As a percentage of net private nonresidential capital

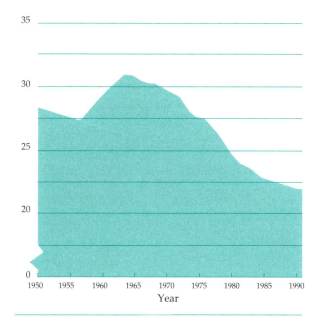

NOTE: Core infrastructure includes highways, airports, sewer and water supply facilities, and electrical and gas generation structures.

SOURCE: U.S. Department of Commerce, Bureau of Economic Analysis

clearly showing a long decline in infrastructure's support of private capital. Some have argued that such a trend is only natural after the major one-time interstate highway construction projects of the 1960s. Yet, the ratio continues to decline well below pre-1960s levels, suggesting that poor infrastructure may be taking a toll on the economy. Studies of certain specific systems confirm this conclusion.[15] Furthermore, cost-benefit analyses indicate that the costs of better maintaining existing infrastructure (coupled with measures to relieve congestion in urban highways and at major airports) are far outweighed by the long-term benefits.[16]

We have already noted that technology plays a critical role in productivity growth. Technological advance is impossible without commitment to research activities, and Federal funding for basic research and development provides a major support for productive innovation by the private sector. As noted in

Chapter 2, private R&D has high private and social returns, indicating that its expansion would be productive. As Figure 20 shows, comparison with other countries also suggests that the United States might productively expand R&D activities. Although the United States spends about as much on R&D as Japan and Germany as a proportion of GDP, and much more in absolute terms, a large proportion of this is defense R&D, which many believe does little to enhance the civilian technology base. Whether or not such "spinoff" is substantial, the coming reduction in overall defense spending is expected to hit defense R&D very hard. Thus Federal policy efforts to raise national R&D spending appear appropriate.

Investments in human resources will also be critical to increases in labor productivity and U.S. competitiveness, and certain Federal programs significantly contribute to this goal.[17] Yet, more Federal dollars for human resource programs do not necessarily increase human capital. For example, the public service employment programs of the late 1970s raised spending levels for "employment and training" activities well above those of more recent

Figure 20

International Comparison of R&D Spending, 1990
As a percentage of GNP

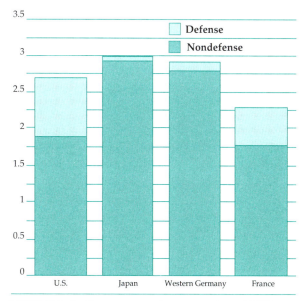

NOTE: Data for France expressed as a percentage of GDP.
SOURCE: National Science Foundation

years. But the fundamental goal of these programs was employment rather than training, and it probably contributed little to the formation of human capital.

Although one can have reservations about the productivity of some public investment-type spending, there can be little question that the composition of Federal expenditures as a whole during the last several decades has shifted substantially toward consumption from investment. And while there are a number of measures which should be taken to improve the quality and productivity of public investments, there appears to be ample room for redressing the balance between consumption and investment in total expenditures.

No discussion of Federal policy and growth can be complete without reference to the effects of regulatory policy, even though these lie outside the immediate budgetary framework of this statement. Environmental, safety, and other regulatory policies are directed at important social goals, and their benefits are not usually included in measures of output and income. However, too often these policies are undertaken without appropriately balancing those benefits with costs; indeed, such comparisons are often excluded from policy considerations by law. It is also often the case that regulatory policies are inefficient, in that greater costs than necessary are incurred to achieve the intended benefits.

These costs can be very substantial. For instance, expenditures necessary to comply with pollution control regulations in the United States were estimated to be $115 billion, or about 2.1 percent of GNP in 1990, up from 0.9 percent in of GNP in 1972.[18] In addition to direct costs, such regulations have indirect adverse effects on long-term economic growth, since they often discourage new investment and innovation. Empirical studies suggest that environmental regulations enacted since 1970 decreased the long-term growth rate of GNP by as much as 0.2-0.3 percentage points, implying that the cumulative loss in potential economic output by 1990 was on the order of $200-300 billion.[19]

Furthermore, many other nonenvironmental economic and social regulations are undertaken by the Federal government. A recent estimate puts the total gross annual cost (exclusive of benefits) of all Federal regulations at around $400 billion.[20] Although study of these broader classes of regulation is very limited, we might reasonably expect that nonenvironmental regulations would add to the reduction of long-term economic growth caused by pollution abatement. It is thus clear that regulations have substantial effects on economic growth. Because these costs are so large, we should take greater care to ensure that regulations are efficient and that their costs are justified by their benefits.

WHY ACTION IS ESSENTIAL:
THE DANGER OF CUMULATIVE DECLINE

One very worrisome aspect of the reduction in national saving, investment, and productivity growth is that the process may become cumulative. Slow growth may generate slower growth — a "vicious circle" of decline. This cumulative process could develop as a result of both economic and political responses.

The economic response revolves around the natural inclination of individuals and families to attempt to maintain their living standards, or their expectations of increases in living standards, in the face of declining or slower growing real incomes. One can hardly fault American families for attempting to preserve their living standards during difficult times, but the likely result is a decline in the private saving rate. Earnings are beginning to fall below those of older cohorts for earners in the same age group. While the decline in the personal saving rate in the last two decades has not been satisfactorily explained, it is probably not coincidental that it occurred during the same period in which average incomes stagnated or fell.

The political response reinforcing slower growth may be similar. As incomes rise slowly or fall, political demands grow for reduced taxes or increased benefit programs to ease the economic pain by maintaining after-tax incomes. This, of course, would reduce *public* saving. It seems likely that the slow income growth of the 1970s and the increase in effective tax rates produced by inflation-driven bracket creep fueled political pressure for the tax reductions of 1981. Similarly, the pressure for tax cuts in the 1992 election campaign may have been related as much to the long-term stagnation of incomes as to the immediate effects of the recent recession.

Although these fears of a cumulative process of reduced saving, investment, and growth are quite speculative, their grounding in common sense is strong enough to cause concern.

The magic of compound growth works in both directions, and a small but permanent reduction in the rate of productivity growth will dramatically reduce incomes and living standards over several decades. It is in the nature of such slow and corrosive changes that action is never imperative but always too late. The possibility of cumulative decline argues for the importance of acting quickly.

Chapter 4

Mobilizing National Resources for Growth

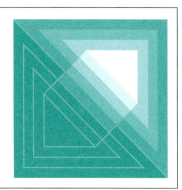

In light of the bias in Federal budget policies towards consumption and against saving and investment, this chapter discusses strategies for mobilizing national resources to increase national saving and private and public investments that will enhance productivity growth and competitiveness. The discussion is organized around the *sources* of productivity growth — physical capital, human capital, and technology — and asks how Federal budget policies might be changed to reignite these engines of growth. The concluding section then addresses the issue of how these budget policies fit into a larger policy framework and what conditions are required to mobilize public support for the necessary policy changes. Before turning to the discussion of specific policies, however, we begin by asking what increases in growth might be feasible and indicate why a variety of policy changes may be required.

GOALS FOR U.S. ECONOMIC GROWTH

As noted in Chapter 1, the importance of raising U.S. productivity growth stems both from domestic and international considerations. Domestically, productivity growth determines the real wages and living standards which form the material core of individual and family well-being. In a world without competing national economies and nation-states, that might be the end of the story. But we do not live in such a world. Indeed, the process of globalization of information, production, and competition have dramatized differences in relative national economic performance. As a realistic political matter, Ameri-

cans will necessarily and properly ask how U.S. growth "stacks up" internationally — in terms of relative and prospective prosperity, the ability of U.S. firms to compete internationally, and the resources available for the United States to maintain its leadership role in preserving international peace and stability.

Setting feasible goals for growth requires some rough assumptions about the growth process and how it might be affected by policy. As Chapter 2 showed, there is widespread agreement that increases in physical capital, human capital, and technology are critical to growth and that increases in some of these productive factors enhance the potency of others. Although there is substantial disagreement about their relative importance, it is clear that *investments* — requiring additional resources generated *by saving* — are necessary to provide any of them. **The uncertainty about their relative importance implies that a growth strategy should not "put all its eggs in one basket," but should contain a diversified set of policies.** And the need to invest resources in each factor affirms the importance of raising national *saving*.

What might be the goals of such a strategy? Looking first at the domestic historical context, Chapter 2 showed that annual U.S. productivity growth averaged about 2 percent in the 60 years prior to World War II. From 1948 to1973, perhaps as a result of special temporary factors, this growth accelerated into the 2.5 to 3 percent range, only to collapse in the 1970s and then rise to about 1 percent in the 1980s. **We should try to raise the annual rate of productivity growth from 1 percent to near its long-term historical average of about 2**

percent. While achieving this goal would not return us to the exceptional growth of the 1950s and 1960s, it would almost double the rate of improvement in living standards over coming decades and do much to reduce the economic squeeze when the baby boomers begin to retire 20 years from now. It is also very ambitious, both economically and politically.

With respect to international competition, the selection of goals is more problematic. Healthy doses of logic and realism are required. The international mobility of technology and capital and implied "convergence" of productivity levels discussed in Chapter 2 logically imply that the gaps in productivity and living standards between most advanced countries will continue to narrow. The technological developments in the United States which support our domestic growth will "spill over" to other countries, and vice versa. Thus, **a narrowing of the gap in productivity growth and living standards, if U.S. productivity growth were strong, would be a U.S. policy success, not a failure**. A central goal of U.S. policy since World War II has been the diffusion of American free enterprise, "know-how," and living standards to other countries. Certainly, we must not regard achievement of that goal as a failure, and we should only applaud if other countries are catching up with a *strong* U.S. performance.

However, we *should* worry deeply if U.S. productivity growth remains so weak that other countries not only converge upon but greatly surpass the productivity, competitiveness, and living standards of the United States. As Figure 21 shows, a continuation of post-1973 productivity trends in the United States, Japan, and Germany would lead to the United States being overtaken by Japan in about 20 years and by Germany in about twice that time.[1] We do not believe that this decline in the U.S. position is consonant with the political expectations of the American people or the international responsibilities of the United States. However, if productivity growth were substantially raised, we might expect gradual convergence among the industrial countries over a much longer period of time, allowing the United States to adjust more gradually, both economically and politically, to its suc-

cess in leading converging international growth in market economies.

How realistic is the goal of roughly doubling U.S. annual productivity growth from its recent rate of about 1 percent to about 2 percent? While the estimates can only be very approximate, this appears to be a feasible but very difficult task, one that requires a major mobilization of national resources and political will. The evidence on the relationship between capital formation and productivity growth suggests that an increase in the net national saving rate of about 5 percent of national income — back to about the 8 percent postwar average prior to 1980 — would raise the annual rate of productivity growth by 0.5 to 1 percent. If that additional saving could then be channeled into the most productive investments, it might be possible to push growth to the top of that range. This indicates the need for growth policies directed at *both saving and investment*: The national saving rate must be raised, *and* that saving must be invested more effectively.

Figure 21

Real GDP Per Worker, Selected Nations
In 1990 U.S. dollars

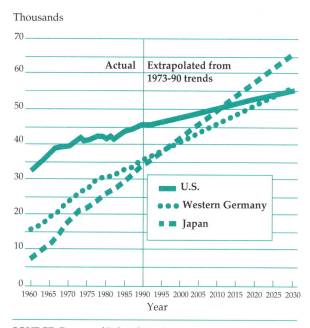

SOURCE: Bureau of Labor Statistics

RAISING NATIONAL SAVING

As explained in Chapter 3, the central feature of the growth slowdown in the United States appears to be the collapse of national saving, related to both higher Federal dissaving through budget deficits and lower private saving. **We believe that a higher national saving rate must become an explicit U.S. policy goal. Public policy should aim to raise the rate of national saving ultimately to its pre-1980 average of about 8 percent of national income — about 5 percentage points above its current level.** While any precise numerical target is arbitrary, an ambitious goal is preferable, as demonstrated by the many years of high saving and growth in such countries as Germany and Japan.

REDUCING FEDERAL DISSAVING: DEFICIT REDUCTION TARGETS

Although the reduction in private saving is not well understood, both the cause of Federal dissaving and its remedy are clear. Federal budget deficits must be sharply reduced and then eliminated. Never before has our government failed to correct policies so obviously destructive of the nation's economic future over such a prolonged period. **The main instrument for increasing national saving must be the reduction and elimination of the Federal structural budget deficit. To reach the national saving target, we should strive for a surplus in the total budget (including Social Security) of about 1 percent of GDP within a decade.** This is the surest and most effective policy to raise national saving and capital formation. By raising future incomes, deficit reduction will alleviate the squeeze on incomes that will be created by the retirement bulge early in the next century and the generational conflict that might accompany it.

As the first step in this process, the deficit should be reduced by an average increment of $50 billion each year for five years, so that in the fifth year the annual structural deficit is about $250 billion less than currently projected. This program should be phased in, and its *implementation* (but not its *enactment*) should depend upon the progress of economic recovery.

This intermediate deficit reduction target is challenging, but certainly not impossible.

Table 3

Federal Spending, Revenue, and Deficit Projections

	Fiscal Years			
Billions of Dollars	**1992**	**1994**	**1998**	**2002**
Revenues	1,092	1,242	1,534	1,870
Outlays	1,382	1,539	1,845	2,384
Deficit	290	296	311	514
Structural Deficit (assuming high employment; excludes deposit insurance, Desert Storm contributions)	218	214	331	524
Debt held by the public	2,999	3,597	4,720	6,461
As a Percentage of GDP				
Revenues	18.7	18.9	19.0	19.0
Outlays	23.6	23.4	22.8	24.2
Deficit	5.0	4.5	3.8	5.2
Structural Deficit (assuming high employment; excludes deposit insurance, Desert Storm contributions)	3.7	3.2	4.1	5.3
Debt held by the public	51.3	54.8	58.3	65.6

SOURCE: Congressional Budget Office as adjusted by CED staff

Table 3 shows the current budget outlook; the structural deficit is currently 3.7 percent of GDP and is projected to remain at about the 4 percent level in 1998. As Table 4 indicates, a $250 billion reduction in the 1998 deficit requires policy changes of 2.2 percent of GDP. The budget program enacted in 1990 required changes of 1.9 percent of GDP. Thus, meeting the intermediate target would require a program roughly 15 percent larger than that of 1990 — a difficult, but hardly insurmountable, task.[2]

The longer term target of a surplus of about 1 percent of GDP by 2002 appears more difficult. The structural deficit rises sharply to more than 5 percent of GDP after 1998, as the cost of health care programs soar. Obviously, reforms in the overall health care system which hold down costs will be required to meet this target. Assuming such reforms, this goal is quite achievable. As Table 4 shows, over this longer period the compounding of lower interest costs has an extremely powerful effect, reducing the politically difficult policy changes required. Thus, if the intermediate 1998 target were met, the longer-term deficit reduction of 6.3 percent of GDP by 2002 would require spending cuts and/or tax increases of less than an additional 2.3 percent of GDP by 2002.

None of this will be easy. As the following discussion suggests, many oxen must be gored. But we must not succumb to the notion that the deficit is "too big for Congress to tame," as though some extraordinary or profound insight were required to find a solution.[3] This is not the situation. We have never been short of *fiscally and economically feasible* choices for eliminating the deficit. Several Administrations, the Congressional Budget Office, the General Accounting Office, and others have produced volumes of options. What has been lacking is political will, both of society and its political representatives. The challenge to political and business leadership is to convince the American people that the real alternative to these unpalatable measures is a future of low productivity growth, low-wage jobs, stagnant incomes, weakened international competitiveness, and a reduced U.S. presence and influence in the world.

To illustrate the point, the table in the Appendix at the end of this chapter provides an illustrative list of proposals which, in vari-

Table 4

Ten Year Deficit Reduction Program

| | Fiscal Years | | | |
Billions of Dollars	1992	1994	1998	2002
Baseline Structural Deficit	218	214	331	524
Policy Changes	–	-32	-179	-447
Interest Savings	–	-10	-71	-171
Total Deficit Reduction	–	-42	-250	-618
Deficit (- is surplus)	218	172	81	-94
As a Percentage of GDP				
Baseline Structural Deficit	3.7	3.3	4.1	5.3
Policy Changes	–	-0.5	-2.2	-4.5
Interest Savings	–	-0.1	-0.9	-1.7
Total Deficit Reduction	–	-0.6	-3.1	-6.3
Deficit (- is surplus)	3.7	2.6	1.0	-1.0

NOTE: Baseline structural deficit from Table 3. Incremental deficit reduction policies average about 0.5 percent of GDP each year in 1994-1998 and 0.75 percent in 1999-2002. Interest savings are based on CBO August basis points initially, rising to 100 basis points over several years.

ous combinations, could meet our deficit reduction goals. *These options do not constitute a recommended program.* The choice of a specific program is ultimately up to elected officials. But the options show both that the problem *can* be solved and that the deficit reduction contributed by most individual proposals is limited enough that in practice a large package of both spending cuts and tax increases would be required to do the job.

REDUCING GOVERNMENT SPENDING: THE GROWTH OF ENTITLEMENTS

A primary line of attack on the budget deficit should be on entitlement and transfer programs, which increase private consumption by raising disposable incomes and public consumption by the direct provision of services. We are well aware of the importance of certain entitlement programs in the national "safety net" and of their role in freeing much of the elderly population from poverty and ill health during the last quarter century. Care must be taken to minimize the effect of entitlement restraints on those with low incomes. But we can no longer afford to fuel consumption by the open-ended growth in programs which transfer vast amounts of resources, largely tax-free, to the middle- and high-income population. This growth of high- and middle-income entitlements has displaced important public investments as well as "safety net" spending. **We do not believe that significant progress to reduce the deficit can be made until entitlement growth is sharply reduced. We therefore applaud efforts to reduce the growth of entitlement spending. However, we urge that entitlement reductions be structured, where feasible, to minimize the impact on low-income beneficiaries.**

Social Security is the largest Federal entitlement program. Changes in the system during the 1980s have generated a substantial surplus which would greatly help to meet our national saving needs were it not being used to finance a gargantuan deficit in the operating budget. Nevertheless, as a matter of both equity and provision for national saving, **we reaffirm CED's earlier recommendations that (A) Social Security benefits should be taxed equivalently to private pensions; and that (B) the** phase-in of the increase in the normal retirement age (and concurrent increase in early retirement) be made more rapidly than current law provides.[4]

Social Security also differs from private pensions in that the latter are not fully indexed to inflation. As a result, many proposals have been made to reduce the indexing of Social Security as a way of reducing expenditures. However, this approach cannot discriminate effectively between recipients with high and low incomes, since the system does not contain the information on incomes required to means-test COLAs. Because many low-income elderly depend heavily or entirely on Social Security, we do not believe that reductions in indexing, which would gradually erode real benefits of retirees, are the best approach to this problem.* **If additional reductions in real benefits are required, explicit adjustments in benefit levels relative to contributions should be made, with due regard to equity considerations.**

We also recognize that the current Social Security incentives for early retirement may not be compatible with the evolving needs of the economy for skilled and experienced workers as the population ages rapidly. The lines between "work" and "retirement" may need to be drawn less sharply, with removal of disincentives to productive activity by older citizens. In this regard, **we favor a liberalization of the earned-income test for Social Security payments if these are taxed like private pensions and when the Federal budget deficit has been brought under control.**

The entitlement programs presenting the gravest threat to our fiscal future are the major health programs: Medicare for the elderly and Medicaid for the low-income population. Each of these programs grew at an annual rate of about 14.5 percent during the last 20 years — almost 9 percent above the general rate of inflation. The outlook, if anything, has now become worse. Over the next decade, under current law, Medicare is projected to grow at an annual rate of 11.3 percent, and Medicaid at 12.8 percent, again 8 to 9 percent faster than general inflation. The share of GDP absorbed by the two programs would rise from 3.4 to 5.8 percent, a 70 percent increase.[5] This program

---

*See memorandum by KATHLEEN FELDSTEIN, (page 57).

growth is by far the most difficult obstacle to deficit reduction. Indeed, once the deposit insurance debacle is behind us, it will become increasingly clear that the "deficit problem" has become in large part a "health care problem." In fact, Medicare and Medicaid are the only major categories of spending (except interest) that are expected to increase as a share of GDP over the next decade under current policies. A recent study by the General Accounting Office (GAO) further suggests that if nothing were done to correct these trends over a longer period, the ensuing deficits would become large enough as to absorb all private saving, perhaps causing economic growth to stop entirely.[6] This, presumably, is not a viable alternative.

We recognize that the problem of exploding health care costs, both public and private, is exceedingly complex and cannot be addressed adequately in this statement.[7] It is obviously not just a public spending problem, since total health care expenditures have now risen to about 14 percent of GDP, a commitment of national resources much higher than in other industrial countries. The nation is, in a very real sense, trading economic growth for massive current consumption of health services that are in many respects inefficient and often abused. A comprehensive reform of health care will involve not only the control of runaway costs but, on the other side of the ledger, the provision of adequate coverage for the 35 million Americans currently lacking it.

While the budget outlook in this area is grim, we are encouraged that health care reform has now moved to the top of the nation's domestic policy agenda. It is vital to the nation's economic future that it be dealt with as quickly as possible. However, we are concerned that some proposals to deal with gaps in coverage may not provide sufficient mechanisms to control costs and/or finance additional public expenditures. **We therefore believe that no proposals for improving health care delivery should be considered unless they contain credible mechanisms for controlling costs and fully financing any additional public expenditures.**

Because Social Security and Medicare account for about two-thirds of all permanent entitlement spending, it is difficult to imagine significant reductions in overall entitlement growth that do not involve these major programs. **Nevertheless, other entitlement programs, such as some subsidies for agriculture and rural electrification, no longer address the problems for which they were created. Many now provide disproportionate benefits to middle- and higher-income beneficiaries. We believe that such programs should be restructured to accord with their original purposes if they remain valid, or otherwise be terminated.**

REDUCING PUBLIC CONSUMPTION

Another line of attack on the Federal deficit must be reductions in public consumption expenditures.

We recognize that some Federal spending involves important investments which may need to be increased. We also recognize that some Federal consumption spending is vital to our economic and social health; the core functions of government administration, the provision of national security, and the foundation of a social "safety net" are essential. Nevertheless, we believe that Federal consumption expenditures for both military and civilian purposes are now larger than appropriate, given their heavy cost in lost economic growth. Our buildup of military spending to current levels reflects a national security threat that no longer exists. Our spending on domestic consumption reflects an expectation about the growth of public resources that is unrealistic. Both must be reduced.

We recognize that the collapse of the former Soviet Union and Warsaw Pact does not mean that the world is benign. The United States must and will remain the preeminent global military power for reasons of both domestic security and world order.[8] Nevertheless, the actual threat to our national security has been enormously reduced since 1989. We cannot afford to waste resources that might otherwise be used to increase economic growth on marginal military purposes that thinly disguise public employment objectives. **Defense expenditures should be reduced to the greatest extent consistent with our new national security requirements, and the** resulting "peace dividend" should go to deficit reduction.[9] **Domestic employment considerations are not an adequate rationale to reject even larger long-term military reductions than those now being planned, and domestic adjustment policies should be enhanced if necessary to facilitate such reductions.**[10]

With regard to Federal domestic spending, **we believe that spending on public consumption can and must be further reduced.** Nondefense discretionary spending has grown in real terms by about 2.5 percent per year for the last 30 years and at about 1.5 percent per year during the last decade, in spite of recent attempts at fiscal restraint. We believe the limits on discretionary spending for fiscal years 1991-1993 established in the 1990 Budget Agreement have been useful and effective. **We strongly urge that any new budget procedures set enforceable limits on discretionary spending after giving full consideration to requirements for infrastructure, education, training, and other productive public investments.** We recognize that some Federal spending for *investment* purposes should be increased to raise productivity growth, but we reject the notion that this requires substantial overall increases in real domestic spending rather than shifting public resources from consumption to investment programs.

Programs for reduction can be identified by asking three questions: Are this program's consumption services more valuable than private or public *investments* of equal cost? If so, does it belong in the public sector rather than the private sector? And, if public expenditures are justified, does it belong in the Federal sector rather than at the state or local government level? Unless all three questions can be answered positively, such expenditures should be reduced or eliminated on an orderly timetable.[11]

Finally, we believe that in light of continually changing national needs, the President is entitled to an "up or down" vote on his requests to Congress to rescind discretionary spending. At present, Congress may effectively ignore such requests. We recognize that the potential expenditure savings from proposed rescissions have not been large historically in terms of the total deficit problem. Neverthe-

less, we believe that such procedures are essential to establishing an attitude and discipline conducive to fiscal restraint and could offer the possibility of significant savings. **We therefore recommend that any new budget procedures include some type of "enhanced rescission" mechanism whereby the Congress is obligated to vote on the President's rescission requests.**

INCREASING REVENUES

We believe that deficit reduction should be undertaken to the greatest extent possible through the reduction of spending rather than through tax increases. However, we also believe, as we stated in 1989, that **carefully designed tax increases that do not discourage private saving and investment will do less harm to the economy than persistent structural budget deficits, provided we have sufficient political discipline to prevent those increased revenues from being spent.**[12] **Therefore, if in spite of a vigorous attempt to cut spending, reductions to meet our budget targets cannot be enacted, deficits should be reduced by raising additional revenues.**

If revenue increases are necessary, certain important principles should be followed. **The burden of taxes will be least if the broadest possible base for taxes is established. Therefore, any additional income tax revenues should be sought first in broadening the tax base by eliminating preferences, where such changes do not reduce national saving. Taxes on consumption should also, in general, be imposed on the broadest possible base.**

The taxation of income and of most goods and services produces inefficient resource allocation; the losses of consumers and others are larger than the revenue raised from the taxes. However, the production and consumption of some goods create social costs which are not reflected in their costs and prices to producers and consumers, but are borne by other members of society. In such cases, taxes which reflect these "external costs" may *improve* rather than harm resource allocation. Clearly, if additional revenues are required to raise national saving, it makes sense to explore possibilities for taxing such products.

Some have argued that such external costs are produced by the effects of tobacco and alcohol on health, safety, and property and of fossil fuel consumption on the environment and climate, urban congestion, and (through large oil imports) national security. However, the measurement of these external costs is extremely difficult, and others have argued that current levels of Federal and state tobacco, alcohol, and motor fuel taxation are already high enough to fully account for such external costs.[13] Thus, in light of current information on these matters, we do not specifically recommend increases in excise taxes on these products. However, **we endorse the principle that, in order to minimize the burden of taxes on society, additional taxes should be considered on the consumption of products which demonstrably generate external health, safety, and environmental costs which exceed current levels of taxation.** We also note that such taxes would fall directly on consumption rather than saving and investment; that the United States taxes these goods much more lightly than most other developed countries; and that the collection of taxes on these goods is administratively simple and inexpensive.

We do not welcome the prospect of higher taxes in the United States. However, we recognize that the severity of the long-term saving and growth problem may make them necessary. We also note that the United States has low taxes *in the aggregate* in comparison with its industrial competitors abroad.[14]

RAISING PRIVATE SAVING

As noted in Chapter 3, the recent collapse in national saving stems from both larger public dissaving and a drop in private saving. The latter is not well understood, although we have speculated that it is related to an attempt to maintain living standards in the face of pressure on household incomes. Whatever the source, the question arises as to whether public policies — normally, tax policies — can be modified to significantly raise private saving.[15] The Congressional hopper is stacked high with proposals for tax incentives which allegedly will raise saving and economic growth.

A healthy skepticism is in order when examining such proposals. The "bottom line" for economic growth is higher *national* saving, not private saving. It is clear that the loss of revenues involved in any tax break *reduces*

national saving unless offset by other tax increases. Only if the increase in private saving exceeds the net revenue loss will *national* saving increase. An increase in national saving is a heavy requirement for any saving incentive to bear. Indeed, there is no strong evidence, amidst much controversy, that saving incentives such as Individual Retirement Accounts and Family Saving Accounts would raise the rate of *national* (as opposed to private) saving.* Such saving incentives might, of course, be financed by other tax increases, but these would impose their own costs.

We believe that the most certain way to increase national saving is to reduce the Federal budget deficit. However, we support private saving incentives that can be shown to raise *national* saving, or that are financed sufficiently to do so.

We also believe that every effort should be made to reduce or eliminate provisions in the income tax code which encourage consumption at the expense of saving and investment. In this regard, we applaud the phaseout of the consumer interest deduction in the 1986 Tax Act. However, we note that this was replaced with provisions for tax deductions of interest on home equity loans, which are advertised and used as a back door mechanism to finance consumption. **We recommend that this subsidy for consumer borrowing through home equity loans be phased out.**

Finally, we note that more radical tax reforms ultimately may be required to increase private and public saving if public saving cannot be sufficiently increased by spending cuts and tax increases under our current tax system. After the recent Japanese tax changes, the United States now remains a singular exception among major industrial countries in not having a value-added tax (VAT). The VAT and other consumption taxes have some shortcomings,[16] and we believe that an extended debate on totally restructuring the tax system might distract the nation from its first, essential task of deficit reduction.** However, if radical reform of the tax system ultimately proves necessary, we believe that serious consideration should then be given to other forms of direct consumption taxation, which might

*See memorandum by KATHLEEN FELDSTEIN, (page 58).

**See memorandum by JAMES Q. RIORDAN, (page 58).

be less regressive and administratively burdensome than a VAT.[17]

Alternatively, private saving and investment could be increased within the framework of the income tax by reducing the additional tax burden on capital income. This might be accomplished by prospectively adjusting net capital income, including interest and dividends as well as capital gains, for inflation and integrating the individual and corporate income taxes to eliminate the double taxation of dividend income.[18] All of this, however, must be done within a framework in which total *national* saving is increased.

The productivity of investment also depends on the ability of business to plan ahead with reasonable certainty. In this regard, **we strongly believe that the tax code should be made more stable. Tax legislation cannot be written in crisis-driven closed-door "summit" meetings. Changes should be made less frequently and through a legislative process which allows for full public hearings and careful Congressional committee deliberation.**

INVESTING NATIONAL SAVING FOR GROWTH

The discussion above has emphasized the importance of national saving — of setting aside a small portion of the resources now being used for consumption for investment in the future. However, a further question remains. If those resources *are* set aside for investment, will they be wisely and effectively used to raise productivity? "Investment" is an attractive label. However, the United States has learned the hard way about unproductive "investments" in both the private and public sectors. The savings and loan debacle (aided and abetted by deficient public policy) saw $250 billion wasted in uneconomic investments, eventually paid for by the U.S. taxpayer. The inefficient use of public monies has also been well documented. However, inefficient investments are not necessarily or even primarily a result of malfeasance, ineptitude, or political influence. Often they result from incentives and biases produced by public policy, and these should be corrected wherever possible.

MAKING PRIVATE INVESTMENT MORE EFFICIENT

As noted in Chapter 3, the current tax system taxes income from business capital much more heavily than income from household capital, of which the major component is residential housing. One recent study estimates that the economic cost of differential tax treatment of capital income (as compared with a policy that treated all capital income the same) is on the order of $2 trillion.[19] This large social cost from diverting investment resources to housing poses a major dilemma for public policy. While the economic loss to society as a whole from this distortion is large, for any individual the tax subsidy is capitalized in the price of housing. Current owners therefore receive little benefit from the subsidy but would face a significant, unanticipated, and arguably unfair capital loss if the subsidy were immediately eliminated. There are essentially two means of reducing this costly distortion between the after-tax returns to business and residential investment:

• Reduce in some manner the deductibility of mortgage interest or (since money is fungible) the deductibility of all household interest. (Current law allows interest deductions on up to two homes on mortgages of up to $1 million.) This has obvious, although diminishing, political problems, and for the equity considerations noted above would have to be done gradually.[20]

• Offset the subsidy to residential investment by countervailing subsidies to productivity-enhancing business investment. This could be done through accelerated depreciation of equipment (as CED has previously recommended)[21] or through the reinstatement of an investment tax credit (ITC) on equipment. Any ITC should be limited to incremental investments above a specified norm, perhaps defined with respect to sales, both to target the subsidy on *additional* investment and to limit revenue costs.[22]

The first approach would be more difficult politically, but it would raise revenue and public saving; the second, in contrast, would lose revenue but would present fewer political problems. It would also respond to recent evidence that the social returns to investment in equipment exceed the private returns, as noted in Chapter 2.

CED recommends that a combination of a tax credit applied to incremental investments* and gradual reduction of the mortgage interest subsidy be used to reduce the costly bias against productivity-enhancing investment in equipment. Tax subsidies for the financing of second homes owned by the same taxpayer should also be phased out.

IMPROVING THE QUALITY OF PUBLIC INVESTMENTS

As noted in Chapter 3, the share of national resources going to investment purposes in the Federal budget has fallen in recent years. More public resources, not necessarily at the Federal level, may be required for infrastructure, education, research, and other investments in growth. However, we do not believe that the size of expenditures is necessarily a good measure of the quality of public investments. We also believe that our public investment requirements will be of a manageable size if we evaluate project returns carefully and set priorities. In that context, we believe that those needs can largely be accommodated by transferring resources from public consumption to investment, rather than by increasing public expenditures as a whole. **As Federal expenditures which raise public and private consumption are reduced, some of these resources should be shifted to public investments in physical, human, and technological capital when the investments can be justified on economic rather than political grounds.**

In many cases, this will involve important changes in the way the Federal government does business. At present, public investments are seldom financed in ways that encourage efficient investment decisions and are often subjected to uneconomic and inappropriate use. Indeed, in some cases it would be unwise to put additional resources into public capital unless the financing and pricing systems were changed.[23] **We recommend that grant formulas for the cost-sharing of infrastructure investments be adjusted to give state and local**

authorities a stronger incentive for rational investment decisions and that pricing mechanisms such as user fees be used more widely to ensure that the use of public capital is appropriately related to economic costs.

The Federal government has traditionally played a major role in supporting basic research as well as applied research in certain areas of "specific priority national need," such as national defense, space exploration, health, agriculture, and the environment.[24] The economic arguments for Federal funding of basic research are compelling. The benefits normally accrue to the society at large and cannot be captured privately, so that investments in basic research with large pay-offs will not be undertaken unless public funding is provided. Recent studies of the growth process have emphasized the critical role that research and technological innovation play in economic growth.

We are concerned that America may begin to lose its once-unchallenged lead in scientific education and basic research. We believe that **Federal support for basic research in our universities should be increased (while subject to stricter accountability) and placed on a more stable and sustainable basis. To ensure that such funds are used productively, the principles of careful professional review should be strengthened, and the recent political "earmarking" of research project funding should be ended.** We are also concerned about the Federal government's allocation of resources in its own research activities. The United States devotes a much higher proportion of its public research monies than other countries to large "high visibility" projects, such as the space station and the superconducting supercollider. **We believe that large public prestige projects with small or highly uncertain contributions to economic productivity should come under closer scrutiny.**

Investments in commercial research also often provide social benefits that exceed the likely private returns, so that a subsidy is appropriate to generate all the research investments with economic payoffs. **We believe that tax incentives for commercial R&D should be strengthened by making the research and experimentation tax credit permanent. Con-**

*See memorandum by FRANKLIN A. LINDSAY, (page 58).

sideration should also be given to more rapid depreciation of investments in R&D.

In general, we support the traditional U.S. division of research labor, in which the Federal government has concentrated its support activities on basic research while commercial research has been left principally to the private sector. However, there is currently concern that the United States is not capturing enough of the economic benefits of its scientific research. The 1993 Federal budget noted that "appropriate Federal investments in applied civilian R&D can result in high payoff to the economy" and has proposed about $17 billion of funding across a wide range of technology areas, including high-performance computing and communications, advanced materials and processing, biotechnology, advanced manufacturing, energy technology, fusion, transportation, and public health.[25]

We recognize that the economic effectiveness of our basic scientific knowledge will increasingly depend upon the capability of our businesses, labor force, government, and other institutions to absorb and employ new technologies productively. We encourage a "capability-enhancing" approach to technology policy [26] — one which does not attempt to "pick winners" but which recognizes that the diffusion and provision of access to new technology is often a public good for which public support will be required to fully realize the potential benefits. **We support careful efforts by the Federal government to facilitate the commercialization of advances in science and technology. However, we believe that the decision process must be protected from political intrusion (as has generally been done in health research) and that the Federal contribution should be limited, with private investment providing the majority of the financing.**

Finally, we underscore the importance of *human* capital— the investments in people that unleash the productive potential of physical capital and technology. CED has long given special attention to education and training and has recently emphasized the importance of a "life-cycle approach to a competitive work force."[27] In addition, we have recently focused on investments in early childhood education and development as a necessary means of realizing the full productive potential of America's increasingly diversified future work force. We will not repeat the specific recommendations on these subjects in this statement. However, we do **emphatically reaffirm the importance of human capital to our overall investment environment. Its quality will go far to determine the type of investments made in the United States and whether investments are made here or abroad.** Those investment decisions ultimately will decide whether our future includes predominately high-productivity, high-wage jobs, or whether we follow a path of lagging productivity and income growth.

PUTTING IT TOGETHER

This policy statement has focused on the Federal budget as a crucial element in our economic growth policies. This stems from the great importance of fiscal policy and the structure of tax and spending policies for national saving and the allocation of investment resources. Nevertheless, budget policy alone cannot do the job; other economic policies must complement budget policy in supporting growth. And finally, the major changes required in budget policy will not be possible without underlying changes in public understanding and leadership that can mobilize public support.

THE OVERALL POLICY ENVIRONMENT

U.S. monetary, trade, and regulatory policies will all have major effects on economic growth, either supporting or working at cross purposes with changes in budget policy. The relationship of monetary policy to budget policy is especially close. The large fiscal deficits of the past decade have placed an additional heavy burden on the Federal Reserve, as unusually high real interest rates have been the inevitable result of monetary policies required to contain inflation. Those high real interest rates have been, in fact, the *mechanism* by which our public dissaving has been transmitted to the economy as lower investment and growth. The first effect, then, of a sound fiscal policy will be to allow the Federal Reserve to conduct a monetary policy more supportive of economic growth as real interest rates come down. We recognize that the major fiscal restraint recommended above will require significant structural adjustments in the economy as resources are transferred from consumption-related to export- and investment-related activities, but we are confident that monetary policy can accommodate those adjustments if fiscal restraint is credible.

A second major concern is trade policy. The United States has led the world during the postwar period in ensuring that trade is a genuine engine of growth, both for itself and the global economy. Rapidly growing trade has been a singular force in realizing the benefits of international specialization and scale economies and in stimulating the transfers of capital and technology that underlie the widening global orbit of market-oriented growth. Nevertheless, there are now strong pressures both in the United States and abroad to look inward for relief and protection from the rigors of global competition and the inevitable conflict over trading practices. There is, therefore, a danger that the process of trade liberalization will be halted or reversed. As we have indicated recently, we believe that these pressures must be strongly resisted.[28] Budget policies to mobilize resources for growth must be supported by trade policies that provide opportunities for realizing that growth potential.

Economic regulation is a third major policy area that impinges closely and directly upon the growth process. Americans have quite naturally and appropriately sought a cleaner environment, reduction of risks to health and safety, and a variety of other amenities as affluence has increased. Nevertheless, the costs of economic regulation in terms of growth and income foregone can be very heavy in some instances, and it is not clear that the public is fully aware of these costs. In some cases, our regulatory mechanisms are not designed to secure environmental or other protection in a cost-effective manner. While we recognize that trade-offs between economic growth (as conventionally measured) and environmental, health, safety, and other regulatory concerns are inevitable, we continue to urge, as in the past, that our political and institutional processes make the costs and benefits of these choices as transparent as possible. Policy makers should continue to develop regulatory mechanisms that will achieve the desired levels of protection at the least cost to society.

LEADERSHIP AND PUBLIC SUPPORT

The budget impasse of the last decade has made it evident that our current political culture does not work effectively to make the difficult and painful decisions required to reduce the deficit and raise national saving. This is not a partisan matter, nor is it attributable to a single branch of government. The roots of the problem extend back into our fiscal history. Nor can we say simply that public leadership has been inattentive and unresponsive to the preferences of political constituents. Indeed, in some respects, our system appears to have become *too* responsive to constituencies, both to the general electorate and to the various interest groups, in terms of short-term political preferences. Entangled in the budget stalemate, we have problems of leadership, followership, and sponsorship, exacerbated by a diffusion of accountability. A resolution of the problem will require actions on all these fronts.

Stronger leadership in making painful political choices certainly will be required, but it perhaps can be exercised effectively only when the public is sufficiently aware of the dangers of our current policies. Interest groups from all sectors of society, while vigorously representing their members, ultimately will have to accept the need for compromise and practice the forbearance required to accommodate it. Finally, other private leaders have a major responsibility to educate the public on the real choices before them so that the leaders who represent them can act effectively in the public interest. CED hopes that this policy statement will contribute to that effort.

Appendix: Illustrative Deficit Reduction Options

All figures in billions of dollars

	Fiscal Years				
	1994	1995	1996	1997	1998
Defense Spending Reductions					
DoD request in FY 1993 Budget	negative saving			0	4
House Armed Services Committee report — midrange option [1]	0	2	8	15	20
"Cooperative Security" defense proposal [2]	0	3	13	32	50
Nondefense Discretionary Spending Reductions					
GAO hybrid package [3]	15	18	21	24	28
User Charges					
GAO hybrid package [3]	11	12	12	13	14
Comprehensive Means-Testing of Entitlements [4]					
All cash and in-kind programs except federal employee pensions	43	48	53	58	62
Civil service and military pensions	9	11	12	13	14
Social Security and Medicare benefit exclusions	22	24	27	29	31
Entitlements Reductions					
Tax Social Security like private pensions [5]	10	24	25	26	27
Phase in higher retirement age more rapidly [6]	4	6	7	10	13
Limit COLAs in non-means-tested benefit programs to CPI minus one percentage point.	3	6	10	13	17
Tax 50% of insurance value of Medicare benefits.	3	10	11	13	15
Align Federal employee retirement benefits more closely with private sector practice [7]	1	2	3	4	5
Reduce farm price supports [8]	0	2	2	3	6

NOTES: Unless otherwise noted, all estimates are adapted from Congressional Budget Office (CBO), *Reducing the Deficit: Spending and Revenue Options* (Washington, DC: CBO, 1992). Budget savings are approximate current dollar declines below the Congressional Budget Office 1992 baseline.

(1) Option C from "An Approach to Sizing American Conventional Forces for the Post-Soviet Era: Four Illustrative Options," House Armed Services Committee Report, February 1992. Actual budgetary data is reported only for beginning and end years; 1995-1997 are extrapolations.

(2) Estimates adapted from William W. Kaufmann, and John D. Steinbruner, *Decisions for Defense: Prospects for a New Order*, (Washington, DC: The Brookings Institution, 1991), pp. 67-76.

(3) The General Accounting Office (GAO) prepared four comprehensive deficit reduction plans with different mixes of spending cuts, tax increases, and user charges. The "hybrid" packages presented here average GAO's high and low options for non-defense discretionary spending cuts and user charges. For more details see GAO, *The Budget Deficit: Outlook, Implications, and Choices* (Washington, DC: GAO, 1990), report OCG-90-5.

(4) Estimates adapted from Neil Howe, "How to Control the Cost of Federal Entitlements: The Argument for Comprehensive Means-Testing," November 1991.

(5) Eliminate current taxable income thresholds ($32,000 for joint filers, $25,000 for single filers) and increase the proportion of benefits subject to tax from 50 to 85 percent.

	Fiscal Years				
	1994	1995	1996	1997	1998
Tax Increases: Broad Based Revenue Sources					
Raise individual marginal rates to 16, 30, and 33% [9]	18	34	37	39	41
Add 38% bracket to above option	7	13	14	14	15
Add a 5% personal and corporate surtax	17	32	34	36	37
Enact 5% VAT (excludes food, housing, medical expenses) [10]	0	45	67	70	74
Tax Increases: Eliminate Certain Tax Expenditures					
Limit mortgage interest deduction to $10,000/$6,000 [11]	7	19	20	21	23
Limit deduction of state and local taxes to 50%	8	21	23	24	26
Limit itemized deductions to 15% bracket value	27	62	66	72	79
Tax employer-paid health insurance above $335/135 per month	10	16	19	22	26
Tax unrealized capital gains at death	*	3	4	5	5
Expand Medicare coverage to all and Social Security coverage to all new state and local employees	2	3	4	4	5
Eliminate Medicare taxable maximum	3	6	6	7	7
Tax Increases: Raise Revenues From Specific Consumption Items					
Double cigarette tax to 48 cents per pack	3	4	4	4	4
Increase alcohol tax to $16 per proof gallon	4	5	5	5	5
Increase motor fuel tax by 25 cents per gallon (phased in)	5	9	14	17	20
Tax all energy consumption at 5% of value	13	17	17	18	19
Tax fossil fuels at $10 per ton of carbon content	8	12	12	13	13

(6) Raise regular and early retirement age three years, phased in over 12 years, and eliminate cost-of-living adjustments during early retirement. CED staff estimates are based on data supplied by the Social Security Administration. Budget savings are augmented by added contributions of workers aged 62-64, who are assumed to continue working until they reach the rising legal early retirement age. Annual saving would be over $30 billion when phase-in is complete.

(7) This option encompasses a host of small changes including deferral and limitation of cost-of-living adjustments and restriction of matching contributions. See CBO, *Reducing the Deficit: Spending and Revenue Options*, pp. 259-261.

(8) This proposal would gradually reduce cash payments made to farmers participating in USDA commodity programs by lowering target price floors for crops by 3 percent per year.

(9) Legislated marginal rates are now 15%, 28%, and 31%.

(10) The revenue effect of this proposal assumes the inclusion of a refundable tax credit to offset the tax up to 150% of poverty thresholds.

(11) Estimates based on data in U.S. Department of the Treasury, Internal Revenue Service, *Statistics of Income—1989* (Washington DC: Government Printing Office, 1992). Current mortgage interest deduction is limited to interest on $1 million of mortgage debt. Capping the deduction at $10,000 (joint filers) and $6,000 (individual filers) would, at today's mortgage rates, allow full deduction on about $125,000 of debt, which is the approximate average size of new mortgages closed in recent years.

Endnotes

CHAPTER 1

1. Committee for Economic Development (CED), *Politics, Tax Cuts and the Peace Dividend* (Washington, DC: CED, 1991).

2. Real GDP is the broadest measure of performance for the economy at large, while after-tax income focuses on the resources available to households. These measures reflect both labor inputs and the productivity of labor. The growth of hourly compensation, as a measure of worker income per unit of "work input," fell more sharply than that of the other measures because the growth of labor inputs rose sharply, and the growth of productivity fell sharply after the early 1970s.

3. Frank Levy and Richard J. Murnane, "U.S. Earnings Levels and Earnings Inequality: A Review of Recent Trends and Proposed Explanations," *Journal of Economic Literatu*re, vol. XXX (September 1992): p. 1338. Increased income inequality does not necessarily imply downward mobility — an actual decline in *specific* individual or family income over time — but makes it more likely.

4. See Laurence J. Kotlikoff, *Generational Accounting: Knowing Who Pays, and When, for What We Spend* (New York, NY: The Free Press, 1992). Kotlikoff estimates that "[u]nless current generations agree to accept a larger share of the costs of paying for the government's spending, future Americans will have to pay at least a 21 percent larger share of their lifetime incomes to the government than is the case of today's young Americans" (p. xiv).

5. Paul Krugman, *The Age of Diminished Expectations: U.S. Economic Policy in the 1990s* (Cambridge, MA: MIT Press, 1992).

6. The *gross* Federal debt is currently about $4 trillion. However, a substantial proportion is held by Federal trust funds — debt that the government "owes to itself." The debt actually owed to the public is about $3 trillion.

7. CED has work under way to analyze the issues in health care reform and assess current proposals, with particular attention to cost control and access.

8. See, for example, *An America That Works: The Life-Cycle Approach to a Competitive Work Force* (New York, NY: CED, 1990), *Investing in Our Children: Business and the Public Schools* (New York, NY: CED, 1987), and *The Unfinished Agenda: A New Vision for Child Development and Education* (New York, NY: CED, 1991).

CHAPTER 2

1. Real wages for production and nonsupervisory workers are a less comprehensive measure of compensation for two principal reasons. First, they exclude managerial and other salaried supervisory workers, who comprise about 20 percent of the labor force. In general, these workers fared much better than production workers in the 1973-1989 period. Second, they exclude employer contributions for Social Security, private pensions, health care, and other fringe benefits. Such noncash benefits have grown as a proportion of total compensation over the entire postwar period. These two factors explain the substantial difference in growth rates between real compensation and real hourly wages. Real hourly wages for production and nonsupervisory workers remain a useful measure, however, since they reflect remuneration for workers popularly considered "blue collar" and do not raise the question of whether larger Social Security contributions and larger health benefits reflect real gains in welfare.

2. For a recent summary, see Frank Levy and Richard C. Michel, *The Economic Future of American Families: Income and Wealth Trends* (Washington, DC: The Urban Institute Press, 1991), Chapter 3.

3. Earnings data from U.S. Bureau of the Census, *Current Population Reports*, Series P-60, various issues.

4. Levy and Michel, *The Economic Future of American Families: Income and Wealth Trends*, pp. 77-78.

5. McKinley L. Blackburn, David E. Bloom, and Richard B. Freeman, "The Declining Economic Position of Less Skilled American Men," in *A Future of Lousy Jobs? The Changing Structure of U.S. Wages*, ed. Gary Burtless (Washington, DC: The Brookings Institution, 1990), p. 35.

6. Computed from estimates in Frank Levy, "Incomes, Families and Living Standards," in *American Living Standards: Threats and Challenges*, eds. Robert E. Litan, Robert Z. Lawrence, and Charles L. Schultze (Washington, DC: The Brookings Institution, 1988) pp. 144, 148-50. This estimate assumes productivity growth of about 1 percent per year. At earlier postwar rates of annual productivity growth of 2.5 to 3 percent, roughly half as much downward mobility would be expected. Recent increases in income and wealth mobility of individual prime age adults are analyzed in Gregory J. Duncan, Timothy M. Smeeding, and Willard Rodgers, "Whither the Middle Class? A Dynamic View," in *Economic Inequality at the Close of the 20th Century*, eds. Dimitri B. Papadimitriou & Edward N. Wolff (New York, NY: MacMillan, forthcoming).

7. "Integration of more low-income households into the economic mainstream will not only help those families gain economic independence, but will also increase the productive resources of the nation and help maintain economic growth." *Annual Report of the Council of Economic Advisers* (Washington, DC: U.S. Government Printing Office, 1992), p. 143.

8. Average family size fell significantly during this period as a result of later marriage and the increasing importance of single-parent families. Official data on family incomes also exclude noncash income and are measured before payment of taxes. For a detailed discussion of corrections for family size, see Congressional Budget Office (CBO), *Trends in Family Income, 1970-1986* (Washington, DC: CBO, February 1988), Chapter 1.

9. Howard N. Fullerton, "Labor Force Projections: The Baby Boom Moves On," *Monthly Labor Review*, vol. 114 (November 1991): p. 31. This smaller labor force will be older (and hence more experienced), somewhat mitigating downward pressures on incomes. However, the effects are very small, since changes in the age structure of the labor force taken alone will likely increase average incomes by only 3 percent over a period of 15 years.

10. Workers provide for retirees directly (by financially supporting relatives or friends) and indirectly (by paying higher taxes into Social Security and Medicare trust funds to finance public benefits).

11. Henry J. Aaron, Gary Burtless, and Barry Bosworth, *Can America Afford to Grow Old?* (Washington, DC: The Brookings Institution, 1989), p. 3.

12. For an excellent description of the fruits of productivity growth, see William J. Baumol, Sue Anne Batey Blackman, and Edward N. Wolff, *Productivity and American Leadership: The Long View* (Cambridge, MA: The MIT Press, 1989), Chapter 3.

13. Baumol, Blackman, and Wolff, *Productivity and American Leadership: The Long View*, p. 228.

14. The uncharacteristic divergence after 1980 is apparently due to the fact that consumer prices (used to calculate real compensation) rose faster than producer prices (used to calculate real output and productivity).

15. Baumol, Blackman, and Wolff, *Productivity and American Leadership: The Long View*, p. 23.

16. George N. Hatsopoulos, Paul Krugman, and Lawrence H. Summers, "U.S. Competitiveness: Beyond the Trade Deficit," *Science,* vol. 252 (July 15, 1988): p. 301.

17. Although assigning particular years as the "start" of a slowdown may seem somewhat arbitrary, the periods analyzed here are generally agreed upon by researchers.

18. For a summary of studies of the 1970s productivity slowdown, see Edward N. Wolff, "The Magnitude and Causes of the Recent Productivity Slowdown in the United States: A Survey of Recent Studies," in *Productivity Growth and U.S. Competitiveness,* eds. William J. Baumol and Kenneth McLennan (New York, NY: Oxford University Press, 1985), Chapter 2.

19. Michael Dertouzos, Richard K. Lester, Robert Solow et al., *Made in America: Regaining the Productive Edge* (Cambridge, MA: The MIT Press, 1989), p. 31.

20. Michael R. Darby, "The U.S. Productivity Slowdown: A Case of Statistical Myopia," *American Economic Review,* vol. 74 (June 1984): pp. 301-322.

21. Although aggregate productivity growth appears to be measured fairly accurately, the *allocation* of this productivity growth among industries is much more problematic. See Martin Neil Baily and Robert J. Gordon, "The Productivity Slowdown, Measurement Issues, and the Explosion of Computer Power," *Brookings Papers on Economic Activity*, vol. 2, eds. William C. Brainard and George L. Perry, (Washington, DC: The Brookings Institution, 1988), pp.347-431. For an alternative approach to the problem, see A. Steven Englander, "Tests for Measurement of Service Sector Productivity," *OECD Science,Technology,and Industry Review*, no. 8 (April 1991): pp. 63-99.

22. John W. Kendrick, "U.S. Productivity Performance in Perspective," *Business Economics,* vol. XXVI (October 1991): p. 7. Since publication of this article, revisions in the estimate of real output by the Department of Commerce resulted in a substantial downward estimate of labor productivity for the 1980s, weakening the evidence for a rebound to the long-term average growth rate.

23. Due to data limitations, international comparisons of productivity are based on output per *worker* rather than the more accurate output per *hour*.

24. In order to compare international productivity levels, data must be converted into a common currency. Market exchange rates do not accurately reflect the relative purchasing power of currencies. This analysis therefore relies on *purchasing power parity* ratios to convert currencies into U.S. dollars, which more accurately reflects real productivity and incomes. See Robert Summers and Alan Heston, "The Penn World Table (Mark 5): An Expanded Set of International Comparisons, 1950-1988, " *Quarterly Journal of Economics*, vol. CVI (May 1991): pp. 335-337.

25. Edward N. Wolff, "Capital Formation and Productivity Growth in the 1970s and 1980s: A Comparative Look at OECD Countries," in *Tools for American Workers: The Role of Machinery and Equipment in Economic Growth* (Washington, DC: American Council for Capital Formation, Center for Policy Research, 1992).

26. Baumol, Blackman, and Wolff, *Productivity and American Leadership: The Long View*, p.103.

27. Some factors thought to have contributed to lagging productivity appear unrelated to public policy, such as pay formulas and other incentives that encourage corporate executives to focus on short-term results. However, such behavior may be largely induced by policy-related high real interest rates.

28. Baumol, Blackman, and Wolff, *Productivity and American Leadership: The Long View*, pp. 262-263.

29. See J. Bradford De Long and Lawrence H. Summers, "Equipment Investment and Economic Growth," *Quarterly Journal of Economics*, vol. CVI (May 1991), and "Equipment Investment and Economic Growth: How Strong is the Nexus?" (paper prepared for the Brookings Panel on Economic Activity, September 1992).

30. For example, see David Aschauer, "Is Public Expenditure Productive?" *Journal of Monetary Economics*, vol. 23 (1989): pp.177-200, and Alicia Munnell, "Why Has Productivity Declined? Productivity and Public Investment," *New England Economic Review*, (January/February 1990): pp. 3-22. For a summary of the debate surrounding this thesis, see Congressional Budget Office (CBO), *How Federal Spending for Infrastructure and Other Public Investments Affects the Economy* (Washington, DC: CBO, July 1991), pp. 23-34.

31. For a summary, see Congressional Budget Office (CBO), *Federal Support for R&D and Innovation* (Washington, DC: CBO, 1984).

32. Edward F. Denison, *Trends in American Economic Growth, 1929-82* (Washington, DC: The Brookings Institution, 1985).

CHAPTER 3

1. *Net investment* is the addition to the nation's capital stock after the deduction of capital that merely replaces capital that is worn out. *Gross investment*, which does not exclude this depreciation, has declined less rapidly than net investment during the same period. The difference is accounted for by the fact that depreciation has grown rapidly because of the increasingly short-lived character of investment, especially in computers. Some argue that the consequent younger age of the capital stock to some extent makes up for the drop in the rate of net investment. *Net domestic product* (NDP) — used synonymously in this statement with *national income* — is the economy's total output of goods and services (gross domestic product or GDP) less depreciation of the capital stock.

2. CED, *Foreign Investment in the United States: What Does It Signal?* (New York, NY: CED, 1990), pp. 21-22.

3. B. Douglas Bernheim, *The Vanishing Nest Egg: Reflections on Saving in America* (New York, NY: Priority Press, 1991), Chapter 3. Some argue that demographic factors — the movement of the large baby boom cohort into traditionally low-saving age brackets — drove the saving collapse, but by that analysis, the saving decline should have begun much earlier than the 1980s. See Barry Bosworth, Gary Burtless, and John Sabelhaus, "The Decline in Saving: Evidence from Household Surveys," *Brookings Papers on Economic Activity*, vol. 1, eds. William C. Brainard and George L. Perry, (Washington, DC: The Brookings Institution, 1991), pp. 194-206.

4. Ethan S. Harris and Charles Steindel, "The Decline in U.S. Saving and Its Implications for Economic Growth," *Federal Reserve Bank of New York Quarterly Review*, vol. 15, no. 3-4 (Winter 1991): p. 15.

5. Charles L. Schultze, "Of Wolves, Termites, and Pussycats, or Why We Should Worry About the Deficit," *The Brookings Review* (Summer 1989): p. 33.

6. In economic terms, "society" — considered as an extension of several generations — would have a discount rate lower than that produced by the market decisions of those currently living.

7. Recent research indicates that certain kinds of investment in machinery which embody new technology may also be such an example. See De Long and Summers, "Equipment Investment and Economic Growth," p. 485.

8. Note, however, that the close linkage between rapidly rising trust fund taxes and spending for Social Security and Medicare weakens the argument that higher spending "caused" the larger deficits. The composition of taxes shifted sharply from income and other taxes to payroll taxes to fund the increased Social Security and Medicare costs; meanwhile, other revenues declined sharply relative to other expenditures. Since the Social Security and Medicare revenues would not have increased except to cover the expenditure increase, one view of the matter is that non-trust fund revenues have been inadequate.

9. Glenn B. Canner, Charles A. Luckett, and Thomas A. Durkin, "Home Equity Lending," *Federal Reserve Bulletin*, vol. 75 (May 1989): p. 337.

10. More accurately, the *combination* of the mortgage interest deduction with the exemption from taxation of the income from owner-occupied housing creates this bias. Were the imputed value of owner-occupied housing services taxable, as a "level playing field" would require, the deduction of mortgage interest as an ordinary business expense would be appropriate.

11. Edwin S. Mills, "Has the U.S. Overinvested in Housing?" *American Real Estate and Urban Economics Association Journal*, vol. 15, no.1 (Spring 1987): p. 613.

12. Dale W. Jorgenson and Kun-Young Yun, "Tax Reform and U.S. Economic Growth," *Journal of Political Economy*, vol. 98, no. 5, part 2 (October 1990).

13. Some have argued that Social Security does not contribute to the Federal deficit and national dissaving because the Social Security trust fund is in surplus. However, the surplus is not a good measure of the degree to which retirement costs are being shifted forward to future generations.

14. Though there is no "official" series of public investment, these data follow the standard procedure of including outlays (including grants to other governments) for physical capital, research and development, and education and training. For a discussion of public investment concepts, see Office of Management and Budget, *Budget of the U.S. Government, FY 1993* (Washington, DC: U.S. Government Printing Office, 1992), Part 3, pp. 35-49.

15. According to one study, the cost in lost output due to automobile congestion alone exceeds $30 billion per year. See James M. Hanks and Timothy Lomax, *Roadway Congestion in Major Urbanized Areas, 1982-1988* (College Station, TX: Texas Transportation Institute, July 1990), pp. 43-58.

16. Congressional Budget Office (CBO), *How Federal Spending for Infrastructure and Other Public Investments Affects the Economy* (Washington, DC: CBO, July 1991), pp. 23-41. Some of the benefits of improved transportation would show up as lower costs and higher productivity as conventionally measured. Other important benefits would accrue in reduced waiting times even where these do not directly reduce costs, e.g., for commuters or shoppers.

17. CED has a long history of support for investment in human resources. The most recent policy statements are *The Unfinished Agenda: A New Vision for Child Development and Education* (New York, NY: CED, 1991) and *An America That Works: The Life-Cycle Approach to a Competitive Work Force* (New York, NY: CED, 1990).

18. Environmental Protection Agency (EPA), *Environmental Investments: The Cost of a Clean Environment* (Washington, DC: U.S. Government Printing Office, December 1990). None of the cost estimates in this section include the effects of the 1990 Clean Air Act amendments. CED will recommend concrete steps to minimize the burden of environmental regulations in a forthcoming policy statement on energy use and the atmosphere.

19. See Michael Hazilla and Raymond J. Kopp, "The Social Costs of Environmental Quality Regulations: A General Equilibrium Analysis," *Journal of Political Economy*, vol. 98, no. 4 (August 1990) and Dale W. Jorgenson and Peter Wilcoxen, "Environmental Regulation and U.S. Economic Growth," *RAND Journal of Economics*, vol. 21, no. 2 (summer 1990).

20. Thomas D. Hopkins, "The Costs of Federal Regulation," paper prepared for the National Chamber Foundation, Washington, DC, 1992.

CHAPTER 4

1. The convergence hypothesis suggests that the differences in productivity growth rates would narrow as convergence proceeds, so that the lines would cross at later dates. However, this effect does not seem to be present yet in the post-1973 data.

2. During the 1980s, Japan reduced its fiscal deficit and indeed moved it into surplus by more than 6 percent of GDP. Germany and the United Kingdom reduced their fiscal deficits by about 4 percent of GDP in moving to fiscal balance. See General Accounting Office (GAO), *Budget Policy: Prompt Action Necessary to Avert Long-Term Damage to the Economy* (Washington, DC: GAO, report number GAO-OCG-92-2, June 1992), Chapter 6.

3. George Hager, "Is the Deficit Now Too Big for Congress to Tame?" *Congressional Quarterly*, vol. 50 (May 2, 1992): pp. 1140-1147.

4. See *Battling America's Budget Deficits* (New York, NY: CED, 1989), p. 31.

5. Congressional Budget Office (CBO), *An Analysis of the President's Budgetary Proposals for Fiscal Year 1993* (Washington, DC: CBO, 1992), Table A-7, p.148.

6. GAO, *Budget Policy: Prompt Action Necessary to Avert Long-Term Damage to the Economy*, pp. 56-62.

7. As noted earlier, CED is currently examining the merits of various health care reform proposals. For background, see CED, *Reforming Health Care: A Market Prescription* (New York, NY: CED, 1987).

8. See CED, *America in the New Global Economy: A Rallier of Nations* (New York, NY: CED, 1992), pp. 8-10.

9. See *The Economy and National Defense: Adjusting to Military Cutbacks in the Post-Cold War E*ra (New York, NY: CED, 1991) This requires clarification. It does not mean that certain domestic investments — for instance, those that CED has supported in education, infrastructure, and R&D — cannot be increased. Its operational meaning is that total deficit reduction must exceed the reduction in defense spending.

10. Defense appropriations for fiscal year 1993 imply a defense spending path moving toward roughly 3.5 percent of GDP by the end of the decade, down from about 5 percent currently. More ambitious "cooperative security" proposals, which would fundamentally alter U.S. military strategy, would produce larger reductions, bringing the defense burden into the range of 2 to 3 percent of GDP by the end of the decade. For a discussion of strategic options, see William M. Kaufmann and John D. Steinbruner, *Decisions for Defense: Prospects for a New Order* (Washington, DC: The Brookings Institution, 1991). The impact of defense spending reductions on the economy is discussed in CED, *The Economy and National Defense: Adjusting to Military Cutbacks in the Post-Cold War Era* and Congressional Budget Office (CBO), *The Economic Effects of Reduced Defense Spending* (Washington, DC: CBO, 1992).

11. The fact that government spending is cut does not necessarily mean that a given service will not be provided at all. There are many cases in which the private sector can and does provide the same service at a lower cost to society.

12. See CED, *Battling America's Budget Deficits* (1989), p. 11.

13. For a recent summary of the evidence, see Congressional Budget Office (CBO), *Federal Taxation of Tobacco, Alcoholic Beverages, and Motor Fuels* (Washington, DC: CBO, 1990), Chapter 4.

14. According to the Organization for Economic Cooperation and Development, total tax revenues in the United States (all levels of government) amounted to about 30 percent of GDP in 1989, about the same as in Japan and far less than the 40 percent average for large Western European nations.

15. Jane G. Gravelle, "Do Individual Retirement Accounts Increase Savings?" *Journal of Economic Perspectives*, vol. 5, no. 2 (spring 1991): pp. 133-148, and Leonard Burman, Joseph Cordes, Larry Ozanne, "IRAs and National Saving," *National Tax Journal*, vol. XLIII (September 1990): pp. 259-283, analyze the evidence. For a contrary view, see Steven F. Venti and David Wise, "Have IRAs Increased U.S. Saving?: Evidence from Consumer Expenditure Surveys," *Quarterly Journal of Economics*, vol. CV (August 1990): pp. 661-198 and their earlier work cited and Martin Feldstein, "The Effects of Tax-Based Incentives on Government Revenue and National Saving," *National Bureau of Economic Research, Working Paper No. 4021*, March 1992.

16. See Congressional Budget Office (CBO), *Effects of Adopting a Value-Added Tax* (Washington, DC: CBO, 1992) and Alan A. Tait, *Value-Added Tax: International Practice and Problems* (Washington, DC: International Monetary Fund, 1988).

17. See David Bradford, *Untangling the Income Tax* (Cambridge, MA: Harvard University Press for CED, 1986); eds. Henry J. Aaron, Harvey Galper, and Joseph Pechman, *Uneasy Compromise: Problems of a Hybrid Income-Consumption Tax* (Washington, DC: The Brookings Institution, 1988).

18. See CED, *Productivity Policy: Key to the Nation's Economic Future* (New York, NY: CED, 1983), p.5. A recent study suggests that full indexation of interest income and deductions would raise rather than reduce total tax revenues. See Roger H. Gordon and Joel Slemrod, "Do We Collect Any Revenue from Taxing Capital Income?" in *Tax Policy and the Economy*, ed. Lawrence H. Summers (Cambridge, MA: The MIT Press, 1988), pp. 89-130. For a fuller discussion of corporate tax integration issues, see U.S. Department of the Treasury, *Integration of the Individual and Corporate Tax System: Taxing Business Income Once* (Washington, DC: U.S. Government Printing Office, 1992).

19. Jorgenson and Yun (p. S-191) estimate that the present discounted value of the lost future production from lower economic growth is $2.7 trillion at a 6% inflation rate. The estimate in the text extrapolates using a lower prospective inflation rate.

20. The increase in the standard deduction after 1986 made itemization of deductions less attractive, especially for middle-income taxpayers. This has two implications: The overall benefit of the mortgage interest deduction has diminished, and those benefits are more likely to accrue to higher-income homeowners. See James M. Poterba, "Taxation and Housing: Old Questions, New Answers," *American Economic Review*, vol. 82, no. 2 (May 1992): pp. 237-242.

21. CED, *Productivity Policy: Key to the Nation's Economic Future* , p. 5.

22. For a description of how such a credit might be designed, see Roger E. Brinner, "A Positive Look at U.S. Economic Prospects and Policies," in DRI/McGraw-Hill, *Review of the U.S. Economy* (December 1991): pp. 37-39.

23. Edward M. Gramlich, "U.S. Infrastructure Needs: Let's Get the Prices Right," paper presented at American Enterprise Institute conference "Infrastructure Needs and Policy Options for the 1990s," Washington, DC, February 4, 1991.

24. CED, *Stimulating Technological Progress* (New York, NY: CED, 1980), pp. 61-63.

25. U.S. Office of Management and Budget, *Budget of the U.S. Government, FY 1993* (Washington, DC: U.S. Government Printing Office, 1992), Part One, pp. 87-116.

26. Lewis M. Branscomb, "Toward a U.S. Technology Policy," *Issues in Science and Technology* (Summer 1991): pp. 50-55.

27. See, for example *An America That Works: The Life-Cycle Approach to a Competitive Work Force* (New York, NY: CED, 1990), *Investing in Our Children: Business and the Public Schools* (New York, NY: CED, 1987), and *The Unfinished Agenda: A New Vision for Child Development and Education* (New York, NY: CED, 1991).

28. See *America in the New Global Economy: A Rallier of Nations* (New York, NY: CED, 1992), Chapter 3.

Memoranda of Comment, Reservation, or Dissent

Page 2, ELMER B. STAATS, with which
JAMES Q. RIORDAN has asked to be
associated.

Any new or additional infrastructure outlays should give first priority to those which are planned and which can be quickly placed under contract; otherwise, inevitable delays may result in little if any impact on the economy in the near term.

Page 4, JAMES Q. RIORDAN

The discussion of studies of trends in the dispersion of income will likely not stand the test of further study and analysis. Recent work has shown that some of the earliest studies were not comprehensive. They were long on rousing rhetoric and short on complete scholarship. Our basic problem is not distribution. It is lack of growth. Concentrating on the politics of "fairness" and envy is not likely to help the new leadership fashion a good plan for growth.

Page 6, JAMES Q. RIORDAN

Reluctantly, I vote against publishing this report. I agree with the report's reaffirmation of our earlier reports regarding the need to reduce the deficit and encourage savings and investment. I disagree with the parts of the report that (a) accept what I believe to be incomplete scholarship and (b) advance new suggestions that I believe will not stand the test of time and have not been fully vetted within the CED.

CED approved an earlier version of this report in May because we assumed that the deficit would not be discussed during the Presidential campaign. We were wrong. The deficit has been discussed at length and all the candidates agreed that the deficit needs to be addressed as a priority item. Having heard the

debate, the country has elected new leadership. The new leadership now needs to translate its campaign promises into a plan of action. That plan cannot do everything at once. It will require tradeoffs.

The CED and its Subcommittees and Boards have no special credentials or mandate to instruct the new leadership in the details of those tradeoffs. CED should be content at this time to remind the new leadership that at all times (including the first 100 days) it needs to keep in focus the long-term objective of reducing the deficit, encouraging savings, and fostering investment that will increase economic and productivity growth. When the new leadership's plan is published, it may be that the CED can provide a service to the nation by evaluating the proposals in light of our long-term objectives.

Page 6, JAMES Q. RIORDAN

There is much in the report (especially the tax proposals) that I hope the new leadership will ignore as it develops its specific proposals.

(a) On balance the report will be read as a call for higher taxes. Based on our recent experience, increased taxation is not likely to reduce the deficit or increase productivity and economic growth. The United States is not taxed too little. Total taxes (federal, state and local) represent a higher percentage of our gross domestic product today than we have heretofore collected in peace time. Comparisons with other countries are misleading to the extent those countries use government to supply certain health, education and other services that are supplied in large part by the private sector in the United States.

(b) The discussion of Social Security in the report is inconsistent. Treatment of Social Security as a private pension (as CED has consistently recommended) includes the taxation of receipts in excess of contributions *but* it also precludes (i) means testing of benefits and (ii) the reduction of benefits for post-retirement age (65) earnings.

(c) The proposals to increase income taxation on those who own their own homes represents a major shift in policy for the country and for CED. It has not been adequately studied and discussed. It may be that careful study will indicate that some changes should be made but our country is not in trouble because too many people own their own homes.

(d) *Incremental* limitations on tax credits to foster investment and research and development will add to the complexity of our tax system. If we want productivity and economic growth, investment and research expenditures should simply not be included in the tax base. There is no effective, simple and equitable way to define a threshold of expenditure that must be exceeded before sound tax policy takes hold.

Page 8, JAMES A. JOHNSON, with which JAMES Q. RIORDAN and LAWRENCE WEINBACH have asked to be associated.

Restoring Prosperity: Budget Choices for Economic Growth is a well-written summary of many of the most serious problems facing the United States in the world economy of the 1990s. It contains many excellent recommendations for increasing investment — both public and private — as well as for cutting the federal budget deficit. There is one point, however, on which no evidence is provided and with which I strongly disagree.

The report claims that there is too much investment in housing and that this alleged overinvestment is caused by overly generous tax subsidies. This implies that tax provisions for housing have helped to reduce productivity and slow the increase in living standards in the United States. The slowdown in productivity growth that began in the early 1970s is not linked — nor has it been linked in any study of this matter, including the CED's — to housing as a cause. Instead, slow productivity growth has been caused by such things as oil price shocks, changing demographics and labor force, a reduction in domestic saving

and investment, and reduced educational attainment. The housing sector receives no more tax assistance, relative to the size of the economy, than it did decades ago. In fact, residential investment is a smaller share of the GDP today than it was 30 years ago. Simply put, investment in housing is not the cause of either the productivity slowdown or the increased federal budget deficit.

This recommendation also is inappropriate because better housing is associated with significant social benefits. There is convincing survey evidence that housing — especially single-family owner-occupied housing — is virtually at the top of households' economic and social goals. There is a strong likelihood that reducing the resources going to housing would permanently exclude from home-ownership minorities and others who historically have been under-represented in housing markets. If housing is not responsible for the productivity slowdown and it delivers large social benefits, then it should not be identified as the solution to these problems — especially by cutting housing resources.

Finally, the statement implies that investment in housing has no productivity-enhancing benefits at all. A major part of any successful urban agenda must include better housing in order to provide a suitable climate for educational attainment by our children. While the impact of better housing on productivity may be both slow in coming and hard to measure, the impact is nonetheless real — and without better education, slow productivity growth will remain a national problem.

Page 42, KATHLEEN FELDSTEIN

I support modifying the annual adjustments to Social Security benefits that now fully compensate for inflation. As a result of this full indexation, Social Security benefits have grown more rapidly than wages during the past decade. By reducing the cost of living adjustment to the excess of inflation over one or two percent, retirees would still be protected from unexpected surges in inflation, while Social Security recipients would share in reducing the budget deficit.

Page 45, KATHLEEN FELDSTEIN

I favor saving incentives and remain convinced by the evidence that Individual Retirement Accounts do increase net national saving.

Page 45, JAMES Q. RIORDAN with which RICHARD J. KRUIZENGA has asked to be associated.

The most unfortunate statement in the report opposes initiatives to restructure our tax system. Our income tax system is a complicated high compliance cost drag on our economy. It encourages consumption and discourages savings and investment. We are fortunate that a number of our political leaders have recently had the courage to call for a radical restructuring of the tax system in ways that would target consumption and spare savings and investment. The initiatives of Senators Nunn/Domenici; Senators Danforth/Boren; Congressman Gibbons and others should be applauded and embraced. The CED should not oppose those initiatives out of fear that facing this problem will "distract the nation." The CED has called for increased taxes on consumption and decreased taxes on income since 1966. We ought not to be afraid of such a change in 1992 when the country has voted its readiness to change.

Page 47, FRANKLIN A. LINDSAY, with which JAMES Q. RIORDAN has asked to be associated.

Prospective indexing of capital gains should be considered as an alternative to an investment tax credit. An investment tax credit has an immediate negative impact on the federal budget, regardless of whether or not the investment ultimately contributes to the economy through increased productivity. It can also distort the quality of investment decisions by providing a subsidy for all investment at the outset, regardless of payout. In contrast, indexing capital gains has a significant impact on the budget only if, and when, the investment begins to return profits to the investor, thereby contributing to productivity and growth. Yet it provides a strong incentive for quality investment by assuring the investor that his real return will be protected from inflationary erosion.

OBJECTIVES OF THE COMMITTEE FOR ECONOMIC DEVELOPMENT

For fifty years, the Committee for Economic Development has been a respected influence on the formation of business and public policy. CED is devoted to these two objectives:

To develop, through objective research and informed discussion, findings and recommendations for private and public policy that will contribute to preserving and strengthening our free society, achieving steady economic growth at high employment and reasonably stable prices, increasing productivity and living standards, providing greater and more equal opportunity for every citizen, and improving the quality of life for all.

To bring about increasing understanding by present and future leaders in business, government, and education, and among concerned citizens, of the importance of these objectives and the ways in which they can be achieved.

CED's work is supported by private voluntary contributions from business and industry, foundations, and individuals. It is independent, nonprofit, nonpartisan, and nonpolitical.

Through this business-academic partnership, CED endeavors to develop policy statements and other research materials that commend themselves as guides to public and business policy; that can be used as texts in college economics and political science courses and in management training courses; that will be considered and discussed by newspaper and magazine editors, columnists, and commentators; and that are distributed abroad to promote better understanding of the American economic system.

CED believes that by enabling business leaders to demonstrate constructively their concern for the general welfare, it is helping business to earn and maintain the national and community respect essential to the successful functioning of the free enterprise capitalist system.

STATEMENTS ON NATIONAL POLICY ISSUED BY THE COMMITTEE FOR ECONOMIC DEVELOPMENT

SELECTED PUBLICATIONS:

The United States in the New Global Economy: A Rallier of Nations *(1992)*

The Economy and National Defense: Adjusting to Cutbacks in the Post-Cold War Era *(1991)*

Politics, Tax Cuts and the Peace Dividend *(1991)*

The Unfinished Agenda: A New Vision for Child Development and Education *(1991)*

Foreign Investment in the United States: What Does It Signal? *(1990)*

An America That Works: The Life-Cycle Approach to a Competitive Work Force *(1990)*

Breaking New Ground in U.S. Trade Policy *(1990)*

Battling America's Budget Deficits *(1989)*

*Strengthening U.S.-Japan Economic Relations *(1989)*

Who Should Be Liable? A Guide to Policy for Dealing with Risk *(1989)*

Investing in America's Future: Challenges and Opportunities for Public Sector Economic Policies *(1988)*

Children in Need: Investment Strategies for the Educationally Disadvantaged *(1987)*

Finance and Third World Economic Growth *(1987)*

Toll of the Twin Deficits *(1987)*

Reforming Health Care: A Market Prescription *(1987)*

Work and Change: Labor Market Adjustment Policies in a Competitive World *(1987)*

Leadership for Dynamic State Economies *(1986)*

Investing in our Children: Business and the Public Schools *(1985)*

Fighting Federal Deficits: The Time for Hard Choices *(1985)*

Strategy for U.S. Industrial Competitiveness *(1984)*

Strengthening the Federal Budget Process: A Requirement for Effective Fiscal Control *(1983)*

Productivity Policy: Key to the Nation's Economic Future *(1983)*

Energy Prices and Public Policy *(1982)*

Public-Private Partnership: An Opportunity for Urban Communities *(1982)*

Reforming Retirement Policies *(1981)*

Transnational Corporations and Developing Countries: New Policies for a Changing World Economy *(1981)*

Fighting Inflation and Rebuilding a Sound Economy *(1980)*

Stimulating Technological Progress (1980)

Helping Insure Our Energy Future: A Program for Developing Synthetic Fuel Redefining
   Government's Role in the Market System (1979)

Improving Management of the Public Work Force: The Challenge to State and Local Government (1978)

Jobs for the Hard-to-Employ: New Directions for a Public-Private Partnership *(1978)*

An Approach to Federal Urban Policy *(1977)*

Key Elements of a National Energy Strategy *(1977)*

Nuclear Energy and National Security *(1976)*

Fighting Inflation and Promoting Growth *(1976)*

Improving Productivity in State and Local Government *(1976)*

*International Economic Consequences of High-Priced Energy *(1975)*

Broadcasting and Cable Television: Policies for Diversity and Change *(1975)*

Achieving Energy Independence *(1974)*

A New U.S. Farm Policy for Changing World Food Needs *(1974)*

Congressional Decision Making for National Security *(1974)*

*Toward a New International Economic System: A Joint Japanese-American View *(1974)*

More Effective Programs for a Cleaner Environment *(1974)*

The Management and Financing of Colleges *(1973)*

Financing the Nation's Housing Needs *(1973)*

Building a National Health-Care System *(1973)*

High Employment Without Inflation: A Positive Program for Economic Stabilization *(1972)*

Reducing Crime and Assuring Justice *(1972)*

Military Manpower and National Security *(1972)*

The United States and the European Community: Policies for a Changing World Economy *(1971)*

Social Responsibilities of Business Corporations *(1971)*

*Statements issued in association with CED counterpart organizations in foreign countries.

CED COUNTERPART ORGANIZATIONS

Close relations exist between the Committee for Economic Development and independent, nonpolitical research organizations in other countries. Such counterpart groups are composed of business executives and scholars and have objectives similar to those of CED, which they pursue by similarly objective methods. CED cooperates with these organizations on research and study projects of common interest to the various countries concerned. This program has resulted in a number of joint policy statements involving such international matters as energy, East-West trade, assistance to developing countries, and the reduction of nontariff barriers to trade.

CE	Circulo de Empresarios Madrid, Spain
CEDA	Committee for Economic Development of Australia Sydney, Australia
CEPES	Vereinigung für Wirtschaftlichen Fortschritt E.V. Frankfurt, Germany
FORUM	Forum de Administradores de Empresas Lisbon, Portugal
IE	Institut de L'Entreprise Brussels, Belgium
IE	Institut de l'Entreprise Paris, France
IEA	Institute of Economic Affairs London, England
IW	Institut der Deutschen Wirtschaft Cologne, Germany
経済同友会	Keizai Doyukai Tokyo, Japan
SNS	Studieförbundet Naringsliv och Samhälle Stockholm, Sweden